Table of Contents

Introduction

In the information technology field one is always having to increase their knowledge and skillset. You are constantly buying books, watching videos, reading blogs, anything you can do to keep current. If anything, there is usually too much information so you get overloaded and have to pick and choose.

A few months ago I was looking to add to my data recovery skills. Not because I was really having problems recovering data, but with Windows 10 and MacOS El Capitan out only a short time and MacOS Sierra being virtually brand new I had not really done much on any of these platforms so I thought a little research would go a long way.

I really wanted a book; Kindle was fine but I wanted to read. I already have more podcasts in queue than I could hope to listen to so that would be a non-starter. Besides, sometimes I just like to sit in the quiet, particularly this time of year when it is seventy degrees and sunny outside. I can sit on my front porch under the eave, drink a glass of lemonade and read. It is very relaxing.

So off to Amazon I went looking for a good book on data recovery. Several popped up and so I bought two and downloaded a sample of the third. I was not happy.

The first book was less than thirty pages and almost half of that was an advertisement and sample section of another of his books. The part that was about data recovery was pretty much a "how you lost your data" section followed by a "list of software recovery tools" section and then a "good luck" section.

The second book was much better but was still really fuzzy on how the data recovery worked, how to find out what happened, and what I could expect to recover. It was however excellent on exactly how to carry out the recovery procedure and the tools he used.

The sample of the third book I downloaded was the worst of the three barely even qualifying for English and having no real usable information for recovering anything.

This got me thinking, what better way to fine tune my skills than to write a book on it myself? It would not just be me telling you what I know, but researching things I don't know, or don't know well enough to explain; I would potentially learn a lot in the process. So here we are.

This book is being written for two different audiences that need a very similar approach: normal people who are not really tech savvy, and budding computer technicians who want to learn about data recovery. I wanted one book that would not only help the average home user, but also kick start someone into being able to do this as a part of their computer business.

I also wanted a book that had not only ways to recover data, but a little explanation behind the hardware and software so you could begin to understand why some data can be recovered and some cannot. Not only that but also a foundation in file storage in general.

Once I got going I had to put in sections on preventing data loss (arguably the single most important section) and making sure data you want gone really is gone. Things always escalate, don't they?

Anyway, I hope you enjoy the book and learn a lot. If you have any comments, good or bad, drop by my website at www.allans-stuff.com and let me know. Both good and bad constructive comments make sure the next version of the book is better than the last so I welcome them.

One thing that I should point out is that it takes a lot of time to put together a book. In this time it is very likely that new versions of software will be released and the screens and options in those new versions may differ from those in this book. Generally the differences are minor enough that you may not even notice. Occasionally the difference are pretty substantial. I have attempted to always use the latest version of the software I am discussing but in the months it takes to write, edit, and finally get it published those may not be the latest version any more. Sorry.

On with the show...

Read this first before doing anything

The first thing you should do, aside from buy this book which you already did, is to turn off your device. Whatever device had the data on it you want to recover, turn that device off. If it was a computer, then turn that off. If it was an external hard drive, unplug that from the computer and power if it has a power plug. If it was a USB flash drive, safely remove it from the computer and put it in a drawer.

The reason for this is that most of the time things only go downhill. Failing hard drives do not heal themselves but instead get progressively harder to recover data from. Files you deleted get things overwritten (you will learn more about this later in the book) making them virtually impossible to recover. Just turn it off.

Later on in the book you will know a lot more and can proceed on the best course of action to mitigate the risks of causing more damage than good.

If you are doing this for someone else, or doing it professionally, make a backup immediately. We will cover cloning and more specifically, bit cloning or full cloning, later in this book and you need to really pay attention to that part. Yes, making a clone of a customer's hard drive takes a lot of time and they will be breathing down your neck to get this done as soon as possible. They will be even more upset if you lose all their data because you didn't make a backup.

I have actually had to have a customer removed by the police from my property at home for something a technician did at my office. Had that technician made a backup, the whole situation would have been avoided.

Even though I say if you are doing this for someone else you should make a clone, I recommend you make that backup even when working on your own equipment. I don't tend to be quite as insistent about it with my own things because I know the risks and know how valuable the data is so it is easy for me to make a calculated and educated decision on whether I want to spend the time making a backup or not. Your customer however will invariably not understand the risks and almost always under or over states the value of the data. Better safe than sorry.

When working inside a device, always use ESD (Electro Static Discharge) safe tools. You know when you walk across the carpet and then touch a door knob only to get that shock? That can kill electronics. By using ESD safe tools and making sure you are grounded (either by using a grounding mat, grounding wrist strap, or really good practices) then you minimize the chances of damaging the electronics. Mats and wrist straps are available from any good electronic store or on amazon.com.

If you wonder if you have "really good practices", you don't. I have spent the last thirty some odd years developing my practices and making them to where they work without even thinking about them, and they are only so-so. If there is even 1% of doubt in your mind, use a strap and/or mat and make absolutely sure.

On occasions you may need to recover data off of an external hard drive. Typically I open the hard drive case, remove the drive, clone it and then do my recovery. I do this because it is faster to clone the drive outside the case and because I have to remove the drive from the enclosure anyway to make sure it is a problem with the drive and not simply a bad enclosure. While most external hard drives are simply internal hard drives mounted in an external case there are two problem types to be aware of.

The first type of issue you may have with an external hard drive is the connector on the hard drive may be directly soldered to a cable, or to a special connector completely different from a standard internal hard drive. These are pretty rare but when they do happen you either have to use them in their enclosure or find a way to adapt or replace their connector with one that will work with a standard hard drive cable.

The second problem is that some of the external hard drives, particularly newer Western Digital drives, may have hardware encryption built into the enclosure. This means that if the drive is removed from the enclosure all the data is encrypted so you cannot read it. I have however been able to remove the drive, do a bit copy of it and then use the new drive in the enclosure for data recovery. I will say that I used an identical Western Digital drive for the target drive to maximize the chance of success and was very surprised that it worked. I expected the encryption to be tied to the serial number of the drive but it was not in my case.

Part 1: What is data loss and what should you do

We will define data as anything on your computer or device that you want to recover. It could be pictures, music, documents, a presentation, or even source code for a piece of software you are writing.

Programs, such as Microsoft Office or Adobe Photoshop are not something you can easily recover as they are not single files or directories. They are very integrated into the operating system (operating systems include Windows, Mac OS X, Android, IOS and Linux as well as others). These typically have a large number of files and folders strewn across the device. You can however sometimes recover an entire hard drive complete with the operating system and applications simply by cloning the drive to another drive.

Now while you may not be able to recover Microsoft Office, you certainly could recover the files that you created and edited with Microsoft Office. That means the newsletter you have been typing on all week could be recovered, as well as the paper you need for your class.

The general idea is that there is one or more files on your device (we will just refer to all computers and devices as a device from here on out) that you want to access and can no longer do so. This may mean that you cannot find the file, cannot open the file if you do find it, or that when opening the file, data is scrambled or missing.

Examples include: a file or files not in the folder where you think they should be, double clicking on a word processing document and it refuses to open or cannot find something to open with, and opening a word processing document and everything inside is scrambled or chunks of text are missing.

There are a variety of reasons why this data may no longer be accessible and we will need to have an idea why it happened before we can come up with the correct way to recover it.

1.1 How data gets lost

You might be one of those people who really doesn't care how the data got lost, you just want it back, and that is perfectly OK. Unfortunately figuring out what happened has a lot to do with figuring out how to get it back. If you simply deleted the file by accident then attempting to replace one of the platters on the inside of the drive will probably only make you lose the rest of your data instead of getting that one file back. Conversely if you have a drive that will not even turn on, it is unlikely that telling you to restore the file from your recycle bin will be very helpful.

Think of it like a car. If the car will not start, replacing the battery when you are just out of gas is not very productive. We need to find out what is going on so we can head down the right path to recovery.

Sometimes knowing what happened is a problem in and of itself. You just open the folder and the file or files are gone. You don't know why, no one knows, and you weren't drinking last night either!

The sections that follow should help you figure out what has happened, explain a little about each type of data loss to help you understand what is going on and then point you to the correct recovery methods to maximize your chances of getting your data back.

1.1.1 Diagnostics

Let's start with the basics, continue down the following diagnostic list until you reach an outcome in all capital letters that matches your specific problem. Then go to that section in the book that matches.

Step 0: Did you delete something you shouldn't have?

If so, the problem is USER ERROR. If not, continue on to step 1.

Step 1: Does the device turn on?

If yes, proceed to step 2. On a computer, check the power cord, any power strip, etc. Plug something else into the same power strip outlet, or wall outlet and see if it works. Check the little switch on the back of the computer (for many desktops but not for laptops) and make sure it is set to 110, 115 or 120 and not to 220 or 240. Test or replace the power supply with a known good unit and repeat the test.

For laptops, remove the battery and try again as sometimes the machine can get "locked up" and removing all sources of power (battery and power adapter) can help unlock it. Removing the battery can also solve a problem where a bad battery such as one with a short in it can keep the entire unit from turning on. You should also try with a different power adapter, even if the little light comes on that is built into the adapter. That little light might only tell you that the adapter is on, not that it has enough voltage or current to power the laptop.

With other devices such as phones or tablets, make sure they are charged or charging. Try a different cable, charger or outlet. I have seen a lot of devices that were "broken" and really only needed a new cable or charger. When my cats were younger they loved to chew USB cables so I was constantly having device issues. A new cable always seemed to fix it, heh.

If you cannot get your device to power on at all you may need to get it repaired before you can continue with your efforts. Desktop and laptop computers, however you can remove the hard drive from them and plug it into another computer to recover your data.

Step 2: Does the device boot up correctly?

If it does, continue to step 4. If not, does it attempt to boot at all? What I mean by this is do you see the Windows, Mac, Linux, IOS or Android start screens? If you see the startup screen but it still does not boot correctly proceed to step 3.

Step 3: Do you hear the drive making audible clicking (or buzzing, screeching, etc.) that it did not used to make, or does the drive fail to spin up at all?

To see if a drive is spinning at all you can usually feel the drive spin when it starts. If not, my old trick was to get a screwdriver and put the bit end on the hard drive and press the handle into my ear (only use this with a large enough handle that it cannot actually enter your ear canal, you want it pressed against the entrance of your ear canal). The screwdriver method allows you to actually hear the motor and platters inside the case without having to open the case.

Of course the best method is to use a stethoscope if you have one laying around. This can be used without having to remove a drive from an external enclosure or from a laptop.

If the answer to either question is a yes, your issue is HARDWARE. If not, run some diagnostic software to make sure the drive is good.

Diagnostic software can usually be downloaded from the hard drive manufacturer. Seagate makes SeaTools and Western Digital makes Data Lifeguard available for free download on their websites in both DOS and Windows versions.

For Macs, some manufacturers still make software that will run on your system but it is not as common. A great solution is Tech Tools Pro from Micromat at www.micromat.com. This is the professional version of the testing software that Apple has included with its computers for years. While it costs $99, this is the software many professionals use to not only diagnose your computer but repair errors and clone drives (more on that later).

An important note is that while a lot of hard drive diagnostics will work if you connect the drive to another computer using USB, the SMART diagnostics built into the drive will not usually be available. SMART stands for Self-Monitoring, Analysis and Reporting Technology and is built into modern hard drives. These drives run the SMART tests and report the results back to the computer at boot (which is why you will sometimes see a warning on boot up of a computer telling you to back up your data because a hard drive failure may be imminent) or to diagnostic software. Unfortunately I have rarely seen SMART data go across USB.

To see the SMART status with diagnostic software, most manufacturer software will check it for you. If you are using other diagnostic software that does not, GSmartControl is a program on the Ultimate Boot CD we will discuss in some detail later in the book. You could also use Parted Magic available from partedmagic.com which includes GSmartControl as well.

If your diagnostics pass, proceed to step 4, otherwise your issue is HARDWARE.

One word of warning here. I have seen more than a few hard drives pass a hardware test and actually be bad. Sometimes it seems it is failing in such a manner that the tests do not test for, and sometimes it seems that it is just barely starting to fail. I will say that 90% of the time I trust the hard drive test software unless something really catches my attention.

So what are some things that might catch my attention and make me not trust the hard drive diagnostics? Drives that are substantially slower than they should be is the most common thing I have seen. I base this off of the speed reported by the diagnostic software, not the speed at which the machine boots or executes tasks. There are far too many factors at play once the machine is booted into an operating system for us to take a speed reading there such as drivers, antivirus background scans and more.

Another thing I have seen that passed the tests but still caused me to replace the drive was while watching the test it seems to pause and then start back up. Sometimes this manifests itself as speeding up and slowing down. The speed the test runs at should be fairly consistent.

In both of these cases I am looking for something obvious. I am not sitting there with a stop watch timing runs and freaking out when one pass is a few seconds slower than another. An example may be that the hard drive is a reasonably newer model that should be giving me speeds well over 100MB/sec and instead I am getting 15MB/sec in a known good machine (don't take the results word for it if it is on the customer's PC because you don't know if their controller and motherboard are good).

Step 4: At the desktop (or whatever the main user screen is on your device), do most things look and work OK and just one file, or a specific group of files is missing as if they had been deleted?

If so, then your problem is most likely SOFTWARE. If not, continue on with step 5.

Step 5: Are your files all there but scrambled when you try to open them? You may also receive a message saying your files have been encrypted or otherwise made unavailable until you do something (usually pay money).

If so you are probably infected with a VIRUS. If not continue to step 6.

Step 6: Do things not operate correctly such as pop ups, unrecognized software or icons on the desktop, etc.?

If so, you probably have a VIRUS or spyware.

Step 7: Look at the capacitors on the system board if there are any (primarily desktops).

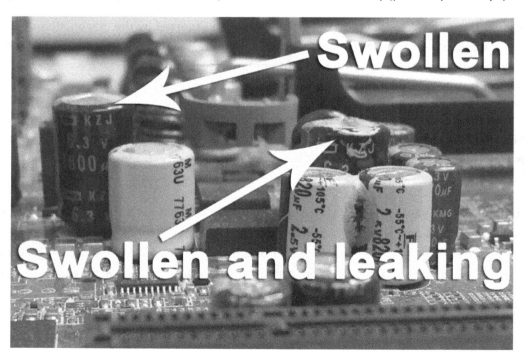

If any of the capacitors are swollen (not flat across the top) and/or are leaking then the motherboard needs to be replaced. This is not really a data recovery issue.

Now that you have been through all the steps, there are some other things to look out for that these diagnostics may have missed. Most of these are just gut feelings.

When I get such a feeling I clone (copy the hard drive from one drive to another using special software) the drive to a new drive and see if things start behaving. One example happened when I was working on one machine that simply would not install or uninstall certain software. Too many things just did not add up with the way the computer was acting and I decided to try a new hard drive even though my diagnostic software said the existing hard drive was good. As soon as the new drive was installed everything started working exactly as you would expect. Software installed and uninstalled normally.

A last place to look in in the operating system logs. In Windows you can go to the Event Viewer and look in the System logs for errors related to the hard drive. If you find them this often means you have a failing hard drive.

So what about hard drive controllers, don't they fail too? Sure. It is far more likely that the drive would fail but it certainly is possible that the controller is causing all the problems. Try the drive in another computer to verify the issue is not the controller.

Hopefully we now have a good idea of what is going on with your data and you can proceed to the correct section of this book to see how you can recover your data.

1.1.2 User errors

User errors are probably the easiest to recover from under normal circumstances. This category includes things such as accidently deleting a file or directory. It certainly can get more extensive than this as I have seen people accidently delete their entire Windows directory (which in and of itself takes some talent to pull off).

Often the files may still be in the recycle bin and can simply be restored from there. Sometimes however people empty the recycle bin without thinking, or have utilities that do it for them automatically, another bad idea.

Believe it or not I have had a customer who actually kept their important files organized inside the recycle bin on a Windows computer. They brought in their machine for a general cleaning and the technician emptied the recycle bin as part of the cleanup. This did not go well as you might imagine. I really wanted to ask that customer if they kept the title to their house and other important documents in their trash can at home but I decided I should keep my mouth closed.

The biggest problem with user errors is getting the user to stop using the machine before the data get overwritten. As soon as you find out you deleted something you need back, stop. From this point on anything you write to the hard drive could overwrite the data you need to recover.

As we will talk about later, when a file is deleted it really isn't. What happens is that the operating system simply marks that section of the storage media as available. Anything that needs to write to the storage media at that point can use that section.

Let's put that a little differently. Say you have a file cabinet and you "delete" everything in the second drawer. The operating system doesn't actually take everything out of that drawer and shred it, that would take too much time. Instead it simply removes the little label on the front of the drawer and replaces it with a label that says "empty" and from then on if you need to put something in the file cabinet it can put it in the second drawer replacing whatever was there and adds the new contents to the new label on the front of the drawer.

If you install new software (for example software to recover the deleted files) it could overwrite the data you need. If you do something as simple as browse the internet your browser is constantly writing files to the hard drive as internet cache and this could overwrite your data. This all assumes that the file you are trying to recover is on the same physical and logical drive (more on those later) as your operating system.

User errors can also extend to things like accidently formatting a drive and erasing all data on it or removing a partition (see Section 2A: Physical versus Logical) completely. These issues delete far more than one file but as long as you stop as soon as possible there is still an excellent chance of getting the data back.

Recovering from these types of issues is best done with the drive removed from the computer if possible and plugged into another computer. This of course is not possible on tablets etc. but we will discuss those in more detail later in the book.

Once connected to another machine, software is typically installed on that machine and run on the drive with the deleted data. The data can then be restored from the mounted drive to the primary drive in this machine so there is no chance that restoring data could overwrite something else you need.

To put this in clearer terms: Remove the drive from computer1 and hook it up as a second drive to computer2. Then install the recovery software on computer2's primary drive. Now run the recovery software and have it look at the second drive (the one you pulled out of computer1). When it finds the data, have it restore it to the primary drive on computer2.

1.1.3 Software errors

Software errors can manifest themselves in many different ways. An example might be that your word processing program might crash and corrupt the file you are working on, or power may fail while you are working on it.

More often than not a software error does not delete a file completely, it just mangles it. What this means is that you can often get most of the information back as a previous version or will lose any formatting such as fonts, spacing, and sometimes even paragraph divisions.

Some files are not really reparable by the end user such as many database files. Typical database files you will have difficulty with on the average user's computer include financial software such as QuickBooks and Peachtree. Both software manufacturers offer services to retrieve your data from corrupt files.

Many programs such as Microsoft's Word include options to open files and recover whatever they can. When opening a file in Word use the drop down box to select "Recover text from any file" as shown here:

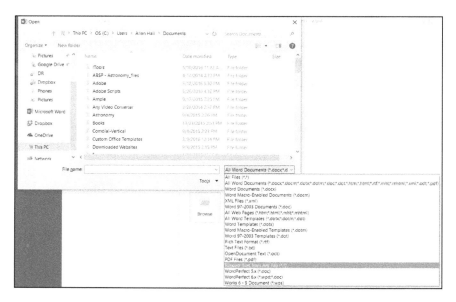

Programs such as Word also may include options to open a file that was not saved. In the case of Word 2013 the button shown in the next image is at the very bottom of the File->Open menu.

Recover Unsaved Documents

One thing to note is that when you run into a situation where the software corrupts the file you need to know why. If it happened because the power failed that is one thing. If it happened because the program or computer locked up, or you do not know why, then you might consider trying to open the file on another computer. It would really stink to try to open your backup only to have it corrupted because the program itself, or computer memory, etc. is bad.

If these options are applicable to your situation then you might try them before actually worrying about dedicated recovery software. Very often the built in recovery solutions work better than the more generic recovery software.

1.1.4 Hardware errors

A hardware error most often occurs when a hard drive fails or starts failing. There are other hardware issues where the hard drive controller has problems, or a cable has a problem, or memory in the computer is corrupting data as it is being written to the hard drive, but these account for an incredibly small percentage of issues. By and large, it's the hard drive.

So what goes wrong with hard drives? Platters can develop bad spots, the heads can "crash" into something and knock them out of alignment or cause damage to them or whatever they crash into, the electronics on the drive's logic board can develop issues, suffer a power spike/brownout or you might break off a pin or connector from the drive. For more information about specific hard drive parts, see the later sections on hard drives.

All hard drives fail, period. They may fail the day they are made, a week later, a year after that or ten years down the road. Hard drives have a mean time between failures (MTBF) which is basically an average. The problem with this is that if there is an average or MTBF of xxxx number of hours of use, odds are a small percentage of drives fail with one hour of use and a small percentage last so long that they never fail from use but are simply retired for larger faster units. Unfortunately a small percentage of millions of drives is not an inconsequential number.

Add to that issue the problem of the companies merging and attempting to lower costs while increasing speed and capacity and you have a recipe for disaster. There are fewer manufacturers of hard drives today than there were ten years ago. Gone are Conner, Maxtor, Quantum and Samsung (all bought by Seagate). IBM's hard drives were sold off to Hitachi which was bought by Western Digital which also acquired SanDisk. Toshiba bought Fujitsu and tons more such as TEAC, Mitsubishi, NEC, JVC, and Iomega either went bankrupt or just left the industry. While all of this was happening speed increased, capacity increased, price decreased and failures increased dramatically.

What once was a fairly rare occurrence, replacing a failed or failing hard drive, has turned into pretty much a daily thing. The only good news here is that slowly SSDs (Solid State Drives) are replacing traditional hard drives.

A SSD is basically just memory that does not require power to remember its data. Memory in a computer normally loses everything in memory when you turn it off, a SSD does not. SSDs are massively faster than normal hard drives and so far have a tremendously lower failure rate. Tremendously lower as in over the past couple of years we have replaced possibly one actually bad SSD (ones that get hit by lightning or flooded don't count) and hundreds of standard hard drives.

The biggest issue I have with hard drives is their tendency to develop bad spots (we call the spots sectors) on the platters. This usually leads to more and more bad sectors which will lead to the drive being totally unusable. Bad sectors can be completely bad in that no data can be written to or read from them, or partially bad in that reading or writing to them take a really long time and may result in an incorrect reading.

All hard drive platters have bad sectors the day they are made. These sectors are marked as bad in a table of bad sectors on the plater itself. Over the life of a hard drive, sectors will continue to fail and as they do the hard drive will simply mark the sector as bad and move on. Drives are made with storage capacity in excess of what they are marked for this very reason.

Once upon a time the bad sectors were marked on a sticker on the top of the drive and were written in ink by hand by an inspector. We have come a long way since then.

Next we have failing heads which is the part that reads data off the drive. Think of a head as the needle and arm of a turntable (if you are old enough to know what that is, although turntables are back in fashion as a retro thing so maybe you do). A bad head can manifest itself as not being able to read or write at all, or that it can read or write but that is slow and error prone. The obvious telltale differentiator between a bad head and bad sectors is that bad sectors typically start with one or two and grow whereas a bad head normally causes a problem to a large percentage of the drive all at once. Since there are normally two heads in a drive for each platter (one on top, one on bottom), this usually does not stop a drive from being usable at all.

Now we come to the logic board on the drive. If you look at the bottom of most hard drives you will see a board with a bunch of electronics on it. This board normally has the connectors on the back of it where you connect your hard drive's data and power cables.

This board controls all the actions of the drive and transfers data from the cable to the heads for writing or from the heads to the cable for reading. There is a little more to it than that but for our purposes the description works.

If the logic board fails it could cause a wide range of issues from the drive not turning on at all to data corruption and much more. Recently we have found a fairly large number of drives with bad cache on them which causes the drive to run extremely slow and corrupt data being read from or written to the drive.

Cache on a hard drive is a small amount of memory installed on the logic board. This memory is substantially faster than the hard drive is capable of reading or writing to the internal platters. Putting memory like this into the drive allows the computer to send data to the drive extremely fast and then the drive can write the data from the cache to the platters inside the drive at a slower rate. This can often make the drive seem substantially faster than it really is. Cache can also be used to read data on certain drives allowing frequently read data to be stored in memory etc.

Cache being faulty is a really annoying problem because I have not found a reliable way to test this problem. What typically happens is I just get a gut feeling, replace the drive and see if the problem goes away. While this works well for repairing a computer it is not really that helpful at recovering data that may have been corrupted by the cache. More on all of this later.

Another hardware error that is possible but far less likely is for the hard drive controller on the computer's motherboard to fail. This controller could even be a separate card plugged into a slot on the motherboard on very old or very high end machines.

1.1.5 Virus/Spyware/Crypto

Cryptolocker, Locky and other ransomware is the single biggest threat to your data today. If you are a business, it is doubly as big a threat. I have seen people lose years of their family photos on their home PC, and multi-location corporations all but shut down. This is nothing to take lightly.

So what is ransomware? Ransomware is a type of malware (unwanted software written by people out to take money from you) that when run on your computer encrypts all of your data (photos, music, videos, documents, spreadsheets, email, etc) so that you can no longer access it. They then give you information on an anonymous way to pay them money for the key to decrypt your data so you can once again access it.

There are two keys needed to decrypt the software, one of which is on your computer and the other is on the bad guy's server. They give you a certain amount of time depending on the type of ransomware such as a forty eight hours, a week or two weeks to pay the ransom. If you do not pay in the given time then they delete the key off their server and then there is no way to ever decrypt your data.

It can not only affect the data on your computer, but on any mounted drive as well. This includes USB drives, external hard drives, and even shared drives on servers or NAS devices.

Isn't this illegal? In the United States, absolutely! Unfortunately both the software and payment methods are largely untraceable so there is no way to find that person. Even if you did find them, the odds are they are in a small third world country where what they are doing may not even be illegal. Even if it was illegal there, there is no way for our law enforcement to do anything about it.

Just recently in the news was a hospital that had to pay thousands of dollars because they could not function, all their data was encrypted including patient files, test results and more. The news has also reported several instances of different law enforcement agencies being hit by ransomware.

So what happens if you pay the ransom? The odds are you will indeed get your data back. As much as I hate to say it, if you do not have backups that were not affected this may be your only choice. Without those backups, even the best computer technician most likely will not be able to get your data back.

To my knowledge, very few people have paid the ransom and not gotten their data back. It is said that the companies behind this ransomware (that's right, this is big business, not some kid in his mother's basement) have established their own technical support departments to assist people who paid in getting their data back. If people paid and didn't get their data back, what motivation would people have to pay?

That hospital that was just in the news and paid thousands in ransom, did they get their data back? Yes. All of it? As far as they have said, yes. Some people have heard that some people paid and didn't get their data back. Yes, and I have heard that the guy down the street was abducted by aliens.

What about those law enforcement agencies? Yes they paid too, and as far as I heard they got their data back. Law enforcement keeps telling you to not pay them, while behind the scenes they pay up just like regular people do. They tell you not to because if this becomes unprofitable for the bad guys they will stop doing it and do something else. Unfortunately if it is your data on the line you might want to do what is best for you and not necessarily what is best for the world overall. Just like they do.

I will say it again, if they did not give you your data back, there would be no incentive for people to pay. They want people to pay, so they tend to fall over themselves making sure you get your data back. If it sounds like I want you to pay them money, that is incorrect. I want you to protect yourself so that you don't have to.

So what if you have backups? A problem with backups is that ransomware can also affect them. If your backup software ran after your files were encrypted, then it backed up useless files. The ransomware could have also encrypted your backups so you cannot restore them. The best types of backups are versioned ones (ones that back up several different copies of each file) and/or ones stored off site. It is also preferable to not use the backup facilities built into your operating system as these are the primary types of backups the ransomware authors will target for encryption.

The best type of backup protection against this would be an automatic cloud based solution such as Carbonite (www.carbonite.com), Sugarsync (www.sugarsync.com) and CrashPlan (www.crashplan.com). This type of software will automatically backup your user data to their servers. Every time a file is changed, it is uploaded to the servers again but that does not overwrite the older version. This way you can restore the file to a state right before it was encrypted and you have lost nothing but a little time.

Cloud backup solutions typically cost between $5 and $10 a month for home users depending on the plan you choose. Business plans that run on servers can be had for a little more money. Keep in mind that for businesses this should be tax deductible and is just as important as any insurance policy you may have.

The next best method is to use a third party backup utility such as EaseUS Todo Backup and backup to external hard drives. Once a week or so swap out the drives and keep the one not being used off site or at least in a fireproof safe. Now if you get hit by ransomware you simply restore the data from the day before you were hit. Keeping a copy off site simply protects you against fire and theft as well as ransomware.

Lastly you could simply copy all your files off to an external hard drive or USB drive manually or using a program such as SyncToy to synchronize the copy to the original. While this is the least preferred method it is still far better than nothing. Just make sure that the data is not encrypted before you copy it to your backup device. You can also increase the protection level by having two backup devices you rotate here as well.

What should you do if you get infected by the ransomware? The first thing to do is turn off any antivirus or antispyware software you may have. Whatever you do, do not run any kind of scan. The reason is as I told you earlier one of the two keys needed to decrypt your data is stored on your computer. If the antivirus removes this key you cannot recover your data even if you pay.

What about taking it to a computer repair shop? Don't bother, there is nothing they can do once you get infected. Sure, they can remove the ransomware and clean up your PC but it is highly unlikely they can get any of your data back. Their solution will most likely be to delete all your data and return the computer to you. They could also want to just reload your operating system and be sure the ransomware is gone. You can do all of this yourself. If you are unsure call your PC manufacturer (for example Dell or HP) and ask them how to restore the PC to factory.

I keep all my data in the cloud, is it safe? Not likely. A lot of cloud services such as Dropbox, Google Drive and iCloud Drive all show up as drives on your computer. Any drive on your computer is likely encrypted. The exception to this is if you access your Google Drive only from Chrome devices such as a Chromebook. Since the ChromeOS will not run the encryption software it is impossible for it to encrypt your data.

If you use an Apple computer you may think you don't have to worry about this. Sorry, wrong. Just recently the Mac program Transmission was hacked to include ransomware on Mac OSX. When you downloaded the program or updated it on the web, it would also install the ransomware. It is true however that this is far less prevalent on Macs than on Windows computers. I expect that to change since virtually no Macs run antivirus or antispyware software and most of the owners think they are invulnerable to this type of attack. Add that with the fact that Macs are more expensive and the bad guys will assume Macs are easy targets with plenty of cash.

How is ransomware delivered to your computer? How do you get infected? By and large through email attachments. You certainly can get infected from software like the Mac just did, or by drive-by web attacks (infected websites), but those are the exception to the rule. I would guess 99% or more of all ransomware attacks I have seen were delivered by email attachments.

So how can you protect yourself from ransomware? First and foremost, do not open email attachments that may be infected. I use this rule: If I am 99.99% sure that it is a legitimate attachment, that is not good enough and I open it on my iPad first. If the attachment opens on my iPad just fine and it is legitimate, then I open it on my PC if I need to. I only open attachments on my PC first if I am 100% sure the attachment is something I should have been sent, and I was expecting it.

I cannot stress this enough, every time you see an attachment are you willing to bet everything stored on your computer that it is legitimate? If the answer is not an instant yes, don't open it. Even a little hesitation, open it on a tablet or phone first.

Next, never download a file you are not sure is safe. Free things on the internet rarely are free. Best case is they may include spyware, malware or PUPs (Potentially Unwanted

Program). Worst case is ransomware may be included as it was on the Mac with the software program Transmission.

You should never turn on "Enable all macros" in your office applications Trust Center. While this does make things a lot more convenient because you won't have to enable macros for programs you know and trust each time you run them, nasty ransomware like Locky which uses Word macros will not be able to run automatically and encrypt everything on your computer and all the computers it is networked to.

It should also go without saying, never download things such as pirated movies, music or software. These are frequently infected. You may think that downloading these on a separate machine with really good antivirus and antispyware protects it. Not so. Many of the people we have seen have had excellent antivirus installed and it acted too late. In addition remember that you are not only putting your machine at risk but potentially every other machine on the same network. This means all machines on your home or business network could potentially be infected.

Once you take all that advice to heart, on a Windows computer you can download a program called CryptoPrevent. This software was written by Foolish IT and is available from www.foolishit.com. This tool isn't magical, it simply prevents executable programs from running from places it really shouldn't. The majority of ransomware runs this way, so this can stop it before it has a chance to encrypt your files.

The CryptoPrevent basic software is free, with paid versions providing automatic upgrades and more features. If you are seriously worried you may do something stupid, I would suggest you pay for the pro version and make sure it was always up to date.

I will state it again for the record, CryptoPrevent is not a magic bullet and will not prevent all occurrences of the Crypto virus. It is an excellent additional line of defense once you do everything else possible to prevent infection.

The antispyware software HitmanPro has released a piece of software called HitmanPro.Alert which says it will not prevent the infection but will prevent the encryption of your data. The software is available from www.surfright.nl and I believe is $24.95 for one year. It is also licensed in a 3 pack and in a 3 year license. Since this solution uses a completely different approach to ransomware protection it could be effectively used in conjunction with CryptoPrevent as a two pronged solution.

One caution: I have heard of a few problems with the HitmanPro solution such as software incompatibilities. Since I do not run the software myself, I would suggest you do a quick internet search just to make sure.

No software is a substitute for good ole common sense and backups but it can work well with them to not only keep you out of trouble, but get you out of a jam when everything fails.

I want to be very clear here. 99.99% of all Crypto infections I have seen were only successful because of the complicity of the user who got infected. There was no magic where it "just happened", someone clicked something or downloaded something they shouldn't have. It is just that simple.

I don't tell you this to belittle people who got infected. These bad guys are really very good at what they do. I do this in the hopes that someone reading this will think twice before doing something that could get them infected and it might save someone a lot of heartache.

1.2 Do it yourself or hire someone?

When deciding to do it yourself or hire someone, the biggest thing to take into consideration is how hard you think it will be to do it yourself and how important the data is to you.

If it is simply a matter of something you deleted that you shouldn't have and it was on a physical device you have access to, then it may not be too difficult. This is the kind of job you should feel fairly confident you can do. If on the other hand your hard drive has stopped spinning at all then this is going to be rather time consuming and difficult, and very unlikely you will be able to recover anything anyway.

How important the data is will be one of those things that only you can decide. Real state-of-the-art clean room data recovery from a failed hard drive can cost two thousand dollars or more. If that number doesn't make you flinch (well, if your reaction is immediately that you would pay that without hesitation) and the job seems complicated or difficult for you to try, then hire a professional.

Let me clarify what I mean when I say hire a professional. I do not mean take it to a large chain electronics store, or to your local computer guy. I mean send it to a company that does data recovery as their primary business, not an add-on service.

So why not take it to the electronics superstore or your local guru who has always done well in the past? Because the truth is they will not be able to do anything you cannot do by reading this book. How do I know this? Over thirty years of experience doing this, this is how I do things at my job, this is how the other techs who work for the same company and other companies I know do this.

There is a huge gap between the typical computer techs and the serious repair centers. This gap includes a real clean room (pressurized area where you are in the all white space suits breathing through oxygen hoses. Ok, maybe not the oxygen hose part.) and hundreds of thousands of dollars in equipment designed to read data directly off the platters of any hard drive on the planet. Most of the techniques used everywhere except these repair centers is at least touched on in this book.

So what kind of data do we send off to the real professionals? Corporate data which could put someone out of business or at least set them in a huge financial burden if they do not get it back would be one great example. Another would be family pictures that were never copied anywhere and now some of the people have passed away so you cannot take new ones. And an unfortunately common one is that someone deleted something to cover their tracks (cheating spouses, illegal activity).

Typical data from accidental deletes and failed hard drives I tend to do in house using the methods I outline in this book. The harsh reality is that most customers will not keep adequate backups and will not want to pay more than a couple hundred dollars total for data recovery. This not only includes the time for recovering the files but the storage medium we recover it to (a new external hard drive or flash drive) and the labor putting it back on their new system.

Occasionally I will attempt recovery in shop and if that fails I will recommend a data recovery service to the customer.

What data recovery services can you use? There are a wide array of them including popular ones like Drive Savers (www.drivesaversdatarecovery.com), Data Recovery Inc. (www.datarecovery.com), ACE Data Recovery (www.datarecovery.net) and Kroll Ontrack (www.krollontrack.com).

1.2.1 Things you may need

When you are working with data recovery, there are certain things you may need to complete the tasks. The obvious thing that jumps to mind is software, and that is true. Software will be discussed in detail later in the book under the correct recovery sections. What you may not think of are things like specialty tools for drive removal and the ability to easily connect the drive to other machines.

The first thing we will discuss is tools. For the typical desktop computer you will need a Phillips head screwdriver or two. Make sure that the screwdriver tip fits securely in the screw to prevent stripping the head which can make it very difficult and messy to remove the screw.

Laptops generally require the same thing as a desktop, a couple of Phillips screwdrivers. These are normally smaller than their desktop counterparts so not only are the screwdrivers smaller, but making sure they fit perfectly in the screw head becomes even more critical. Laptops can also be difficult to get into without a selection of pry bars.

One note is that Apple computers often require special screwdrivers to remove some of their screws. A torx set can be very useful although most of the time three bits will suffice: T4, T6 and T8.

Devices such as phones and tablets can get a little more involved if you need to disassemble them. Fortunately this is very rare as removing the storage drive from them really is normally not worth the trouble. Tools for these include not only small and specialized screwdrivers such as pentalobe bits, but a significant number and style of pry bars.

A great toolkit for disassembling virtually any small device (laptops, tablets, phones, etc.) is the "iFixit Pro Tech Toolkit All New 2016 Edition" available from ifixit.com or on amazon.com. This has a wonderful set of bits to fit anything including game consoles and high security devices and also has excellent pry bars, tweezers, spudgers (plastic things to poke and prod with), a suction cup for screen removal and more, all in a nice carry case and all for less than $100.

The only tool I would add to this toolkit for small devices is an iSesamo. This is a thin flexible tool ideal for prying apart small cases or working into the edge to release latches.

For larger devices I prefer full sized screwdrivers. If you are doing this professionally, use professional screwdrivers such as Xcelite, Whia or Klien. Using these high grade tools will allow you to work faster (as they slip less), damage fewer screws and remove already damaged screws. Believe it or not they can actually save you a considerable amount of money even though they cost more initially. The Xcelite ESD (Electro Static Discharge) safe models are a personal favorite for electronic work.

Assuming you are working on hard drives you may need to connect that drive to another computer to run diagnostics or recover data. You could of course open the second computer and install the drive inside but there are easier and faster ways. The first is a device such as the Vantec CB-ISATAU2 SATA/IDE to USB 2.0 Adapter. This has a cable that plugs into the hard drive and then into an available USB port, then a separate power adapter much like a laptop power adapter. This should allow you to attach any IDE or SATA hard drive from either a desktop or laptop computer to the USB port of any other desktop or laptop computer. Hard to beat when it is available on amazon.com for around $15.

This is really nice if you are doing this professionally as you only need your laptop on site to start working on the customer's hard drive.

The next option is the Thermaltake BlacX Duet 5G ST0022U which is a little box that sits on your desk and plugs into the wall for power and an available USB3 port on your computer. Hard drives are then simply plugged into the top of the device (up to two hard drives at once, either laptop or desktop drives in either bay) and then you turn on the device. This is an excellent solution for your repair bench although it is reasonably small and light so it certainly can be used mobile as well.

If you are working with memory cards such as SD cards, try the Sabrent USB 3.0 Super Speed 4 slot Memory Card Reader for Windows, Mac and Linux. This little guy can read SD , SDHC , SDXC , MMC / MicroSD , T-Flash / MS , MS PRO Duo / CF, and more all for around $10 from amazon.com. Not only is it cheap and flexible, but it is really fast as well.

1.2.1.1 Making bootable media

Booting to CD/DVD is fairly simple process, all you need is a bootable CD/DVD. If you are looking for free solutions for Windows you can grab a copy of the Ultimate Boot CD (UBCD) from www.ultimatebootcd.com. Not only is this a great little bootable CD but it contains quite a few diagnostic tools including many of the hard drive manufacturer's own tools, and several cloning tools including the free version of HDClone. This may be a fantastic solution for the home user or even technicians just starting out.

UBCD and many other bootable utilities are distributed in ISOs. These are basically images of discs, a single file that contains all the files and necessary data to create a CD/DVD/flash drive or other form of media. Think of it as a clone of a drive in a single file. You could also think of it this way, making a clone of a hard drive is like making a Xerox copy of a document while making an ISO is like scanning the document into a computer.

You might be asking how to make a bootable CD from the ISO, and that is an excellent question. We will discuss that next.

1.2.1.1.1 Creating a bootable CD/USB in Windows

I like to use a free program called ImgBurn (www.imgburn.com) for Windows for creating bootable CDs. This is a really fast and easy program for doing a lot of things with CD/DVD discs and images but is perfectly suited for this task. Download and install the software to a computer (not the one you need to get data off of) and then run it.

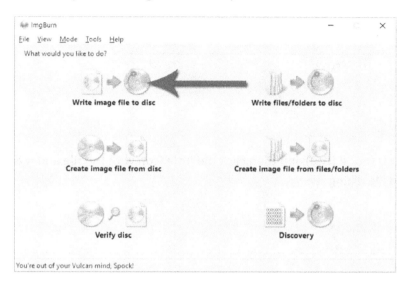

Select the first option "Write image file to disc".

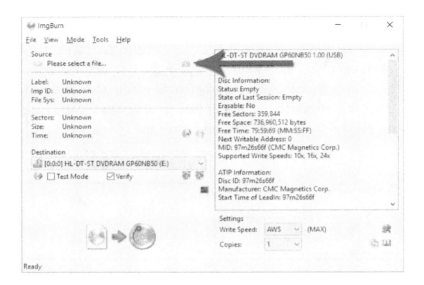

Insert a blank CD (not a DVD) and then click the little icon with the file and magnifying glass to bring up the file dialog box.

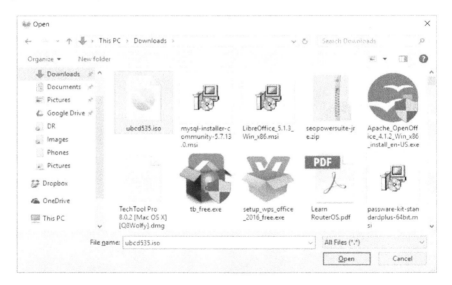

Browse to and select the ISO image for UBCD you downloaded, highlight it and click Open.

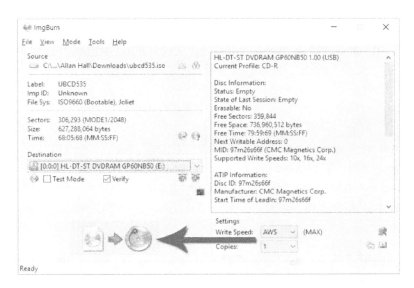

Now click the big icon on the bottom left of the screen of the file folder, arrow and CD. Wait a couple minutes and you should be done.

What if you do not have a working CD/DVD drive, or you just want things faster and easier? Boot to USB instead! The same UBCD will allow you to create a bootable USB flash drive you can boot to instead.

The first step is to download a program called WinRAR (www.rarlabs.com). This program is available as a free trial (and if you just need to do this one thing that works fine), for free with TrialPay or for $29. Install the program on a computer (again, not the one you are trying to recover data from). Now find the UBCD file you downloaded in Windows explorer and right click on it. Now select the "Extract to UBCD535\" (where the 535 is the version you are working with) from the menu that pops up.

Now open a command prompt (pressing the Windows key and typing "CMD" will display a link which you can click on to open a command prompt) and type the following commands:

```
cd downloads\ubcd535\ubcd\tools\win32\ubcd2usb
```

```
ubcd2usb c:\ubcd-extracted x: /f
```

These commands assume you are using Windows Vista, 7, 8 or 10 and that you downloaded the file into your default downloads directory and lastly that the version of UBCD you downloaded and extracted was 535. If you are using a newer version of UBCD, then replace the numbers in the command line above where it says 535 with your version number and it should work.

The second command above assumes that x: is the drive letter of the USB drive that you want to make bootable. You can find out the drive letter by opening the file explorer and looking for the USB drive you plugged in. Whatever that drive letter is, that is the letter you should put where the x is.

In the image above my USB drive is D: so I would type:

```
ubcd2usb c:\ubcd-extracted d: /f
```

Also note that the "/f" on the end of the command tells it to format the USB drive, deleting everything on it. Make sure the drive does not contain any data you want to keep before running this command.

On a Mac things are a little different for UBCD. First, since Macs are basically an offshoot of Linux (for you technical people out there FreeBSD, I know) a lot of what works on Linux works on Mac when booted to a Linux environment. Since UBCD boots to Linux, a lot of it will work. Different users report different successes and failures. If you already have UBCD or really want to try it, go for it.

The good news is that you can clone a Mac hard drive using a PC with the UBCD, or with HDClone installed under Windows. You can also clone the active hard drive in a Mac using any of the Mac tools we discussed earlier such as CCC, SuperDuper or even Apple's built in Disk Utility.

I have had problems with the latest HDClone and Mac drives running El Capitan. My theory is that it seems to work when the drives are the same size but fails going from one size drive to another. I have no doubt that Milray will fix this little issue, in fact probably before you read this, but do be prepared just in case.

Lastly, Tech Tools Pro will let you boot to their Edrive (their software once installed allows you to make a bootable USB flash drive, they call this Edrive) and run diagnostics, repairs and even clones from that device. Nice.

As a technician, my personal favorite solution is to clone everything on a Windows PC using the Thermaltake BlackX adapter and HDClone Professional when possible. This provides a single solution with the greatest flexibility. If the clone is expected to take some time, I use this setup on a bench machine (a bench machine is usually a desktop computer sitting on the technician's workbench used for just such things) otherwise I may use my laptop or even the customer's own PC booting from my USB flash drive.

1.2.1.1.2 Creating a bootable CD/USB in MacOS

MacOS makes burning an ISO such as the UBCD pretty much a trivial process, if you have an optical drive. I say if because depending on your computer, you may not have one built in. My iMac does not but I have a USB DVDRW I swap between the iMac and my laptop as needed.

Once you download the ISO and load a blank CDR in your drive simply open up your downloads folder in the finder and right click on the filename. On the menu that pops up select Burn Disk Image… as shown in the following screenshot.

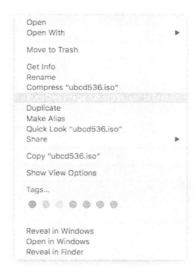

MacOS will pop up the next screen to make sure you want to proceed, click the Burn button.

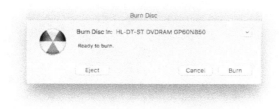

MacOS will start burning the image to the disc.

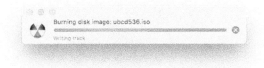

Once the process is complete, the system will verify the disc and then eject it closing the program in the process. Easy peasy.

With a Mac you typically want to boot the machine to an installation media such as MacOS. These install media typically have disk utilities built in for rudimentary diagnostics and repairs.

To create a bootable USB drive for MacOS Sierra you can download the Sierra installer from the Mac App store on any working Mac. Then you can download a free program called Install Disk Creator (macdaddy.io/install-disk-creator/). Unzip the Install Disk Creator and double click the app.

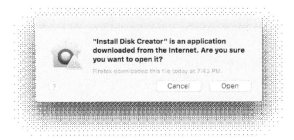

Of course select Open from the warning box that pops up.

Use the box at the top of the screen to select your USB drive. Keep in mind that anything on the USB drive will be erased and that the drive should be at least 8GB in size.

Since you have already downloaded the Sierra installer it appears in the box below the USB drive. Click the blue Create Installer button to begin.

Enter your password and click the blue button OK.

The blue status bar will start to move across the bottom showing you the progress. This could be pretty quick if you have a USB 3 port and a fast USB 3 drive, or if using slower equipment this could take quite a while, so be patient.

Once complete you will see the screen above. Click the blue OK button, eject the USB, and insert it into the machine you want to boot to it on, hold down the Option key and select the USB drive.

1.2.1.1.3 Creating a bootable CD/USB in Linux

Assuming you have a fairly up to date (in the past few years) distribution of Linux this could not be too much easier as they typically have everything you need built right in. We will be using Ubuntu 16.04 LTS for this.

Download UBCD or whatever disc image you want to burn to CD. Launch Brasero which is installed by default in Ubuntu.

Over on the right side you will see the image you downloaded listed, click on it.

On the next screen that comes up click the Burn button.

Brasero will start burning the disc and show you the progress as well as the speed.

Once completed Brasero will tell you if it was successful and allow you to make more copies or close the window.

Making a USB drive is a little more complex but you start by downloading the ISO like we just did above. Here I am using Ubuntu 14.04 LTS. Open your download folder and right click on the iso you downloaded.

Select Open With and Archive Manager.

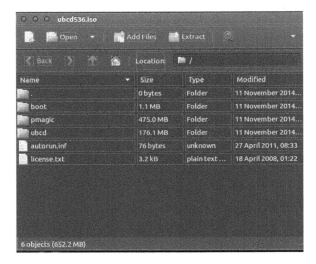

Now click the button in the top center that has a folder icon and says Extract.

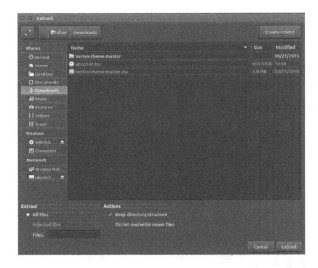

I just extract here since I have very little in my downloads folder or you can use the Create Folder button near the top right to create a folder to hold the extracted files in. Once you are happy with where the extraction will take place click Extract on the bottom right.

Now you can click the center button for Show the Files. Now we need to navigate to the downloads/ubcd/tools/linux/ folder assuming you extracted directly into your downloads folder. There is a readme.txt file you need to read regarding making certain scripts executable if you are running GNU/Linux.

Now navigate to the downloads/ubcd/tools/linux/ubcd2usb/ and open the redme.txt file for step by step instructions on how to make a bootable UBCD USB drive. These instructions use tools and paths that are dependent on the UBCD distribution and could change so I opted to have you read the readme for instructions instead of including them here.

1.2.2 Making a copy or clone

Before you begin, especially if you are doing this for a customer or the data is critical, you should make a backup. When doing data recovery you need a special kind of backup called a bit copy or full copy clone (from here on out I may refer to this as a bit clone).

When data is deleted off a drive it is not actually removed. What happens is the area of the drive where that data is stored is marked as empty by the operating system. If you just do a normal backup it will not backup space that is marked as empty.

A clone uses special software to make an exact copy of a drive. Think of it as a Xerox machine for drives. The problem is that like a Xerox machine if there is nothing on a particular part of the page (a spot marked as empty on the drive) it does not copy it. The solution to this is a bit copy clone.

The difference between a standard clone and a bit copy clone is that where a standard clone only copies sections of the drive with data on it (sections marked as not empty) the bit copy copies every single part of the hard drive regardless of what anything says is or is not there. This ensures that deleted data is copied as well.

Using a bit copy clone (which I am going to start calling just a clone from now on so my fingers don't fall off) allows us to try a variety of recovery techniques with minimal risk to the original drive. Why do I say minimal instead of no risk? Because even making one clone of a failing drive is risky, but far less risky than not doing it.

So how do we make a clone of a hard drive?

The first thing is you have to have a target drive to clone the source drive to. The source drive is the drive that you are trying to recover data from. Your target drive must be at least as big as the total amount of data on the source drive. To make this easier just make sure that the target drive is at least as large as or larger than the source drive. By large I am referring to its storage capacity.

Next we need some software to make the clone, which we will discuss in detail in upcoming sections.

One package for this is HDClone which comes in several versions, including a free non-commercial version. The free version does not currently do Mac or server drives, is restricted to 2TB or smaller drives and is slower than the professional version. If you are doing this commercially, then I suggest you buy the professional version at around $95 as it will do pretty much anything you ever wanted and do it fast.

Another excellent program is EaseUS Todo Backup which also comes in several versions. The nice part about this software is that the free version has none of the limitations of the HDClone free version and has a nice easy-to-use interface. It does not have as many cloning options so before you decide to purchase it make sure it has everything you need. For most professionals it is more than sufficient. It does however have a lot of capabilities such as backups that are not really HDClone's forte.

EaseUS also makes Disk Copy in both free and technician versions which is simply a cloning tool that has its own Linux boot media. If all you need is cloning and you do not have another PC to install software onto then this may be an excellent option. With the Linux boot media you can clone using just the one PC without booting into Windows and running the risk of overwriting data you may need to recover.

Lastly for PCs there is Parted Magic (www.partedmagic.com) which has diagnostics, cloning, data rescue and data secure delete built into one bootable CD or USB flash drive. While not free, at only $9 this is an excellent program with a nice feature set that can do a lot for very little.

For Mac users, Carbon Copy Cloner (CCC) is the gold standard in hard drive cloning. SuperDuper is another excellent program although as of this writing I do not believe it will clone the restore partition on newer Macs so I will put it in second place. While CCC is $40 and worth every penny, SuperDuper has a free version that is perfect for home users and a commercial version that is only $28 which unlocks all the more advanced features.

The good news for some Mac users is that Apple stuck in a feature in its Disk Utility starting in OS 10.3, cloning. This feature was removed a couple of years later so the newest versions of MacOS unfortunately do not have it. While I do not think it does a true bit copy, it is certainly better than nothing and it is free if you have the right OS version. This is probably best used for failing hard drives where you can still get a good copy before it dies.

For something a little more capable there is Tech Tools Pro. This software has extensive diagnostics, not just for the hard drive but for the file system and even the entire computer. It comes on a bootable DVD making it very nice if you ever need to run diagnostics or do a clone and cannot boot to the hard drive in the Mac. What it lacks in advanced cloning features it more than makes up for with other tools and abilities.

For either Windows or MacOS you could also use a device such as the Kingwin USB 3.0 to SATA and IDE Adapter with the One Touch Clone feature. These standalone clone devices run about $32 from Amazon and allow you to do a bit clone from any IDE or SATA drive to another drive of equal or larger size. It does MacOS, Windows, Linux and pretty much anything you can plug into it, all without software or the need to connect it to a computer. At this price you could have a few of these laying around so you could do clones without taking up a bench PC.

Now we need to connect the source and target drives to a secondary computer either internally or using one of the adapters discussed in the previous section, connect the target drive to the original computer or use the standalone clone device.

If you connect the target drive to the original computer you cannot boot to the default internal hard drive and make a clone of that drive to the target. Said another way, the source drive cannot be the boot drive and cannot be active in any way. The solution to this, if you must use the original computer, is to boot to something other than the internal hard drive.

Today there are two basic ways to accomplish this, booting to CD/DVD or booting to something like a USB flash drive. If you do this professionally you may also be able to boot to a PXE server (a special computer on the network that allows you to use it as a boot device) but this is not something most individuals or even small shops have.

1.2.2.1 HDClone (Windows/Mac)

HDClone, available from www.hdclone.com, comes in a variety of different editions from free through enterprise editions. For typical home users, the free edition will probably be more than sufficient. Technicians should consider the advanced edition at a minimum (it is the lowest edition with Apple drive support) or more likely the professional edition as it is the lowest edition to support servers.

Once the software is installed on your computer (not the computer you need to make a clone of, of course) running it brings up the main menu.

From this main screen select Drive on the center far left under Cloning. You can also use the Bitcopy function to the right if both your source and target drives are identical.

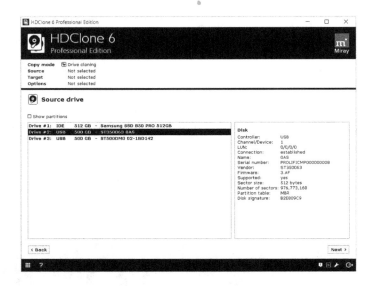

Now you need to select the source drive or the drive you are making the copy of by clicking on it and then clicking on Next in the lower right.

This screen allows you to select the target drive or the drive you want to make into a copy of the source drive. You can click on the drive you want as the target and then click on Next in the lower right.

Here is the options screen which you typically do not need to deal with when you are making a copy for upgrading or replacing a hard drive in a computer. For making a full copy (what I usually call a bit copy but HDClone has a bit copy mode so I don't want to confuse the two) be sure the Smart Copy feature in the upper left is unchecked.

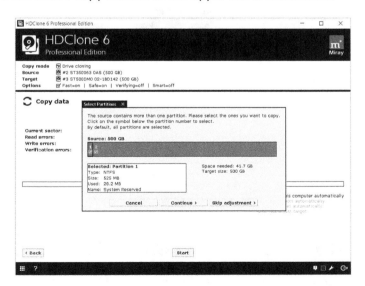

Now you will see a partition selection box like this and can typically click on Continue in the center.

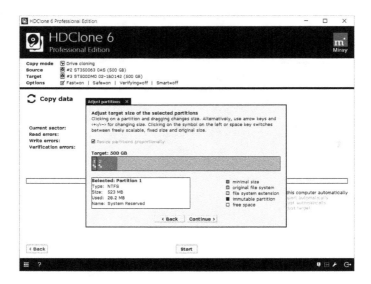

Next this pop up may appear asking you how you want to adjust the partitions if the source and target drives are not the same size. Leaving this set to automatic and clicking Continue is the normal operation.

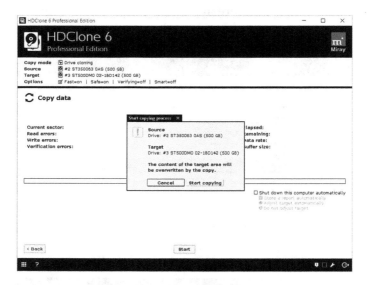

The next box asks you to verify the settings for the copy. Here you should double check the source and target drives and then click the Start copying button.

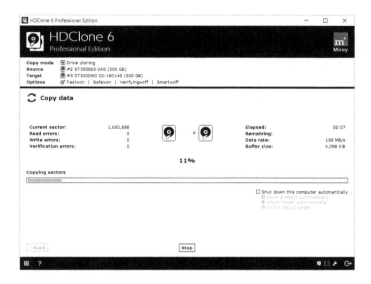

After a couple of minutes it should start the copy giving you an estimate of the amount of time left to complete the copy.

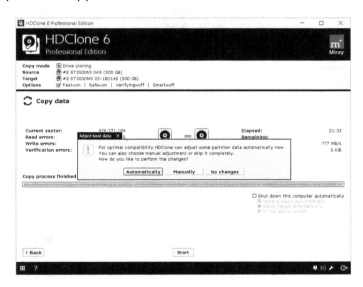

Now you will see another pop up asking you if you want HDClone to adjust the boot data. Typically you will click on Automatically.

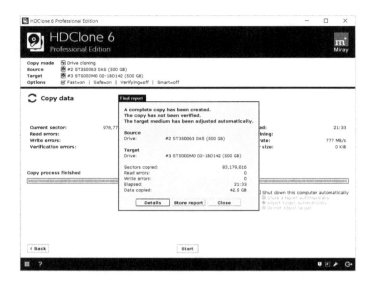

Once the copy is complete HDClone will present you with a report like this one.

If you are making a clone of a failing hard drive you may see read errors such as in this image. The more read errors, the longer the copy will take and the less likely you are to get a fully working drive with all files intact.

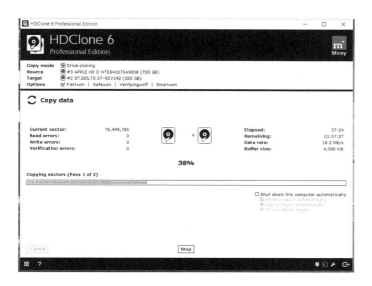

If you start to see write errors like in this image you need to worry that your target drive may be bad. I have also had issues with things not being plugged in completely causing this. If you get write errors and think the drive is good, unplug everything, shut down the computer, and redo everything from scratch. I have had this fix problems several times. Of course your target drive may just be bad, even brand new from the store. The last possible cause of this is if the source drive is really bad it can actually cause errors on the write as the computer has a hard time switching speeds from the source to the target.

That should be it. Note that a full copy will take substantially longer than a standard copy as the copy process copies not only the data but all the empty areas (where deleted data is stored) as well.

1.2.2.2 EaseUS Todo Backup (Windows)

EaseUS Todo Backup (www.easeus.com) is a nice little free program which can do drive cloning similar to HDClone. The primary differences between the free version and paid versions is the addition of support and faster transfers on the paid versions.

Once the program is downloaded and installed simply run it to get the main menu.

At the main menu you will need to select the Clone button to the right of center near the top.

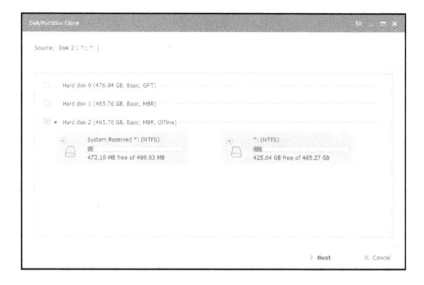

This screen allows you to select the source drive, or the drive you want to make the copy of. Check the box next to the drive you want to copy and then click Next in the lower right.

Here you select the target disk and make sure to check the box near the bottom labeled Sector by sector clone.

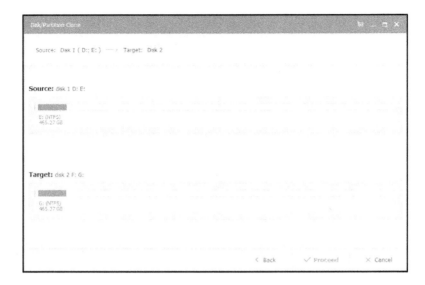

This screen allows you to verify your options before the cloning begins. If you are sure, click on Proceed.

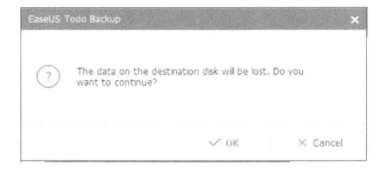

One last time it will ask you if you are sure, click Ok.

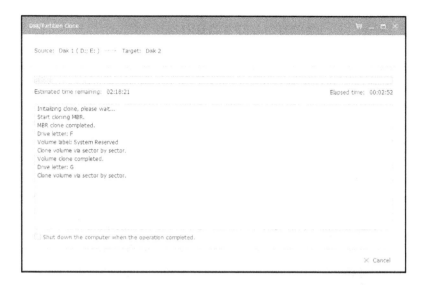

Once the clone starts you will see the progress and estimated time to completion displayed here.

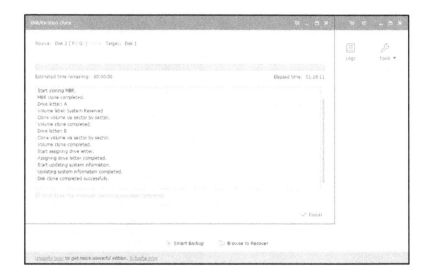

Now that the copy is complete, click on Finish.

1.2.2.3 Clonezilla (Windows/Linux)

If you are working on a Windows or Linux PC using the UBCD we discussed earlier, then we can use Partition Magic on the UBCD to make a clone. This actually runs a program called Clonezilla to make the clone.

Insert the UBCD disc we discussed earlier and boot from it.

Select Parted Magic from the menu of options.

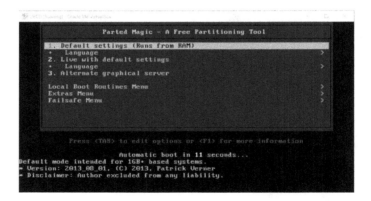

You can just press enter to accept the default settings.

You will see a lot of text scrolling on the screen as the software loads.

After it boots UBCD will ask for your time zone.

Double click on the Disk Cloning icon right on the desktop to launch Clonezilla.

Clonezilla starts up and gives you two options; the top option of working with images or the bottom option of working directly with disks. Since we are making a clone we will be selecting the bottom option and press the enter key.

I almost always select the first option on this screen; disk_to_local_disk. This is the option that allows you to work with two hard drives (or SSDs, or combinations of SSDs and HDDS) connected directly to one computer which is the case for me 90% of the time.

The other three options allow you to copy just partitions, or to copy disks and partitions to a remote computer instead of the one you are working on. Select the option you want and press the enter key.

Now we get a screen that displays all the disks we can work with. If you are making a clone there should be at least two. If there is only one you should stop and double check all your connections to make sure that the drives are working correctly.

Note that you need to reboot the computer and restart both UBCD and Clonezilla after making sure the connections are good.

Select the drive that will be the source, or the one you want to make a copy of and then press the enter key.

The next screen shows a list of available drives to clone to, or to be the target. Since there were only two drives and the first one was the source, only one shows up here. If you had three drives connected to the computer then there might have been three on the first selection screen and two on this screen so be careful in your selection. Select the target drive (if not already selected) and press the enter key.

This screen shows three options; copy without repairing or checking, copy and ask you what to do along the way, and copy and attempt to check and repair the disk before copying. The top choice is the default and the one I use most often. Select one and press the enter key.

Clonezilla now switches to a command line and starts asking questions. This first one simply asks are you sure while telling you that your operation will overwrite all data on the target drive. This gives you a chance to back out if you are not sure.

Press the "y" key and then the enter key.

WARNING!!! WARNING!!! WARNING!!!
WARNING! THE EXISTING DATA IN THIS HARDDISK/PARTITION(S) WILL BE OVERWRITTEN! ALL EXISTING DATA WILL BE LOST: sdc
Are you sure you want to continue? ? (y/n) ▊

Again it displays a warning and asks if you are sure. Press the "y" key and then the enter key to continue.

Do you want to clone the boot loader (executable code area, the first 446 bytes) to: sdc ?
[Y/n] ▊

This question asks if you want to copy the boot loader so the target drive will be bootable. You will only see this if the source drive is bootable to begin with and since I want an exact copy I press the "y" key and then the enter key.

Now we will start to clone data to the target machine...
Are you sure you want to continue? ? (y/n) ▊

One final time it wants you to confirm the copy. Press the "y" key and then the enter key.

Clonezilla now begins the copy process and shows you the progress.

```
Ending /usr/sbin/ocs-onthefly at 2016-10-17 14:53:02 CDT...
Press "Enter" to continue......█
```

Once the copy is done it switches back to a command prompt and tells you to press the enter key to continue. Once you do that it will exit back to the Parted Magic desktop as if nothing happened so this is its way of letting you know everything is complete.

Your clone should now be complete so you can turn off the computer, disconnect the drives and continue on with your job.

1.2.2.4 SuperDuper (Mac)

SuperDuper (www.shirt-pocket.com) is an excellent program for making a clone of Mac hard drives on a Mac. The free version will do everything most people will need from the software. Their paid version is $28 and allows scheduling, automatic updates and scripting. If you are a home user using the software once or twice for clones, then I would just use the free version. If you plan on doing this professionally or need the extra features then I suggest you go ahead and get the paid version.

One issue you may run into is that SuperDuper does not work with a totally empty target disk. If you purchase a new hard drive and want to use it for cloning, you first need to use Disk Utility in the Mac's Utilities folder to erase the disk. This will create the partition and filesystem you need.

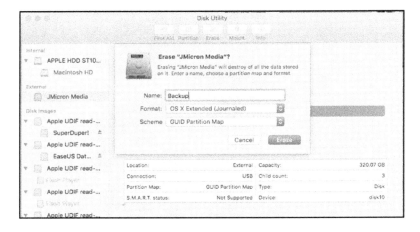

You can name the drive whatever you like. The Format should be set to "OS X Extended (Journaled)" and the Scheme should be "GUID Partition Map". Click Erase and let Disk Utility do its thing.

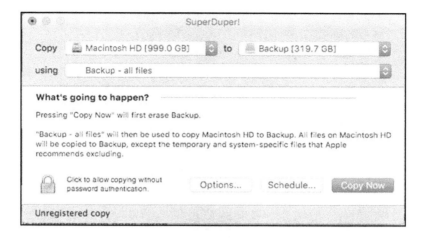

Now you can run SuperDuper. Select your drives on the top (you can make a clone of your boot drive while you are using it, or any other attached drive). Your source drive is on the left and target on the right. The drop down box below that should be set to "Backup - all files". Double check your selections and click "Copy Now".

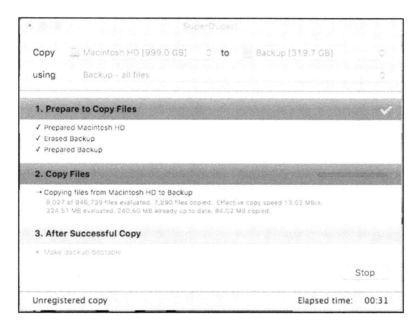

The next screen will show your copy progress along with other statistics such as amount of data to copy and the current copy speed.

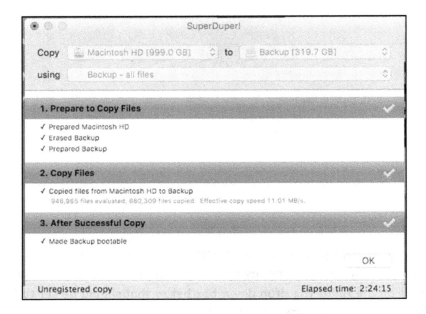

Eventually you will see the completed screen showing what all was done. This clone was on an iMac i5 with 8GB of RAM with not a lot of data on the hard drive across USB. A faster connection method such as Thunderbolt would have increased the speed of the backup. The backup also takes a longer time than you might expect because it is copying data that is currently on a hard drive while it is being used.

If you need to update a clone, the copy process will be much faster as it will only copy files that have been added or changed since the last time you made a clone.

SuperDuper has been an excellent program and made copies even when others have failed.

Part 2: Understanding data storage

Data is stored digitally, that is in ones and zeros. This can be represented in many different ways but the result is the same, a string of ones and zeros that the computer can understand.

What we need to know is a little more in depth so that we understand what we can and cannot recover, and how to maximize the odds of getting all our data back. You certainly would not want to polish the surface of a hard drive platter but that may be an excellent solution to certain problems with optical media. If you don't understand the way these media types work, you may have no idea why.

The following sections attempt to walk you through the different types of physical media storage and then the logical storage schemes present on the different types of media.

2.1 Physical versus logical

There are two different types of divisions of storage, physical and logical.

Physical is just what it sounds like, a physical object. This can be a hard drive, flash drive, optical disc, floppy disk, etc. It is an object and refers to the entire object.

A logical device or drive is a division of the physical device and is often referred to as a partition. For example a single physical hard drive can be divided into one or many different logical drives.

Think of a physical drive as a file cabinet drawer, and the file folders inside as logical drives. On computers running the Windows operating system each logical drive is referred to by a drive letter. Think of each file folder in the file cabinet drawer as a folder with a letter on it. You stick all the documents for John Smith in the folder labeled S for Smith. All the document for Bobby Jones goes in the folder J, and so on.

There are many reasons you may want to have multiple logical drives on a single physical drive including protection from filling up a critical section with non-critical data, divisions of different data types, etc.

A good example of this occurring is most new Windows based computers ship with a single storage device (either a hard drive or SSD) and this one physical device is divided into several logical devices. These logical devices typically include: a boot management partition that contains information about what partitions have operating systems and are bootable, a restore partition which allows you to boot to this partition and reload Windows should something happen to the OS, and lastly the actual operating system partition which you use on a daily basis.

A server might have some of the same logical partitions as the computer described above but also include one or more partitions reserved for data storage and sharing. These are separated from the boot drives so that if the users fill up the data partitions it does not also fill up the partition with the operating system which would cause the entire computer to crash.

2.2 Media

Media is the object or device that data is stored on. These include hard drives, USB flash drives, SSDs, CDs, DVDs, and in the past even audio cassettes and floppy disks. Technically even a piece of paper is media but not really relevant other than as an illustration of the point.

All media will eventually fail for one reason or another. Hard drives have incredibly small tolerances with high speeds and heat which breaks them down. SSDs, flash drives, SD cards etc. have a finite number of times they can be written to. Optical discs degrade over time due to the dyes used breaking down. Even stone tablets will erode from running water and air pollutants. You just can't win.

Understanding how the media works, its limitations and structures, will help you be better prepared to recover data, and to protect your data from loss in the first place.

2.2.1 Hard drives

Hard drives are incredible little devices. When you look at one it just seems like this little block of metal and plastic. It has enough weight in desktop size to be used quite effectively as a small hammer, and is small and light enough in laptop sizes to carry comfortably in a shirt pocket.

The reality of what it does and how it does it might actually take you by surprise. I know the first time it was explained to me I was just amazed that it worked at all.

Let's start with the physical outside and work inside. My description and pictures will be primarily of a desktop hard drive but smaller drives such as those found in a laptop are very similar, just smaller. Just as an aside, there are even smaller hard drives than the ones in laptops called microdrives. These were often used in cameras, digital audio recorder/players and other very small devices.

The outside of a modern hard drive is crafted from primarily aluminum. What you see turning one around in your hand is a chunk of aluminum with a circuit board on the bottom with connectors on the end and a metal screw-on cover where they affix the drive label.

Looking at both the circuit board and cover you often see that the screws holding these in place are not standard Phillips or flat head screws but often hex or torx. These are probably done because both of these types of screws are superior to standard screws and allow for a high degree of accuracy in not only tightening but also placement. If you have ever tried to put a standard flat head or Phillips screw on the tip of a screwdriver and have it stay while you inserted the screw in a hole you know why they may want to go to a different tip; it doesn't tend to fall out as much. With delicate work like this, every advantage helps.

It is also possible they like to do this to keep people from messing with it, although I highly doubt this. If you went in and messed up your hard drive you would have to buy a new one, which has no down side for the manufacturer.

The tool set I recommended under the "Things you may need" section will have everything you need to disassemble any hard drive I have ever seen. I will say however, do not ever disassemble a hard drive you are not prepared to lose everything on. Read on to find out why.

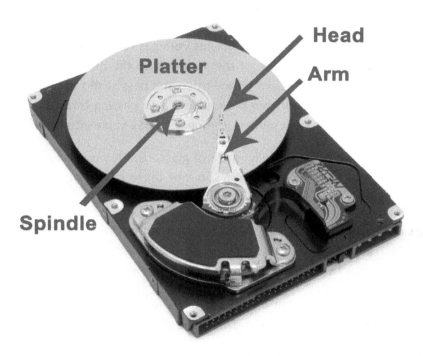

After removing the cover off the hard drive you will see two main components: the platters and the head/arm assembly. The platters are the big round things that look like small records on a record player. The head/arm assembly looks like a tone arm and needle assembly for a record player. There is also usually a smaller circuit board inside the drive.

I was a bit worried about making reference to a record player because that is very old technology and I was not really sure the younger generation would get the references. It seems however that vinyl is making a comeback as I see albums in stores and online more often now than in the past ten years. Funny how that happens.

A hard drive works much like a record player, only it can also record. The heads move back and forth over the surface of the spinning platters and read data. Records accomplish this by lands and pits. A simplified description is that when the needle hits these irregularities in the vinyl album it creates a noise which is then amplified and played out your speakers.

A hard drive is very similar but uses magnetism to read and write pieces of data to the spinning platters. The heads can either passively read the bits of data as it passes under the head, or change the data on the drive by applying voltages to the head causing a magnetic field which can change the orientation of the data bits on the platter. The data read can then be processed by the circuit board on the drive and passed through the data cable to the computer much like the audio from the record player passing through the RCA cables into your stereo (or on some newer models, through the USB cable into your computer).

The platters in a hard drive are typically made of glass, ceramic or aluminum coated with several very thin layers of other materials. Some of these layers include insulators, the primary cobalt magnetic layer and even a lubrication layer on the very top.

These platters can spin at 5,400, 7,200, 10,000 or even more revolutions per minute. Faster spindle speeds (so called because they spin around a spindle) typically mean a faster drive. There is one other factor that determines the raw speed of a drive and that is areal density.

Each microscopic data storage area on the platter is magnetized either one direction or another representing either a one or zero. This single piece of information is called a bit.

The areal density is a measure in bits per square inch (BPSI) of how much data can be stored on a platter. The higher the areal density, the tighter the bits are packed onto the platter and the faster they can be read at a given speed. If for example you had two drives both spinning at the same 7,200 RPM with one drive having an areal density of around 2.25 billion BPSI and the second drive with a 5.5 billion BPSI, the second drive could read approximately twice as much data in the same amount of time as the first drive.

The heads are used to either read data off the platters using Faraday's law or to change the orientation of the magnetic particle using magnetic induction shifting the value from a zero to a one, or one to a zero.

Wikipedia describes Faraday's law of induction as a basic law of electromagnetism predicting how a magnetic field will interact with an electric circuit to produce an electromotive force—a phenomenon called electromagnetic induction. It is the fundamental operating principle of transformers, inductors, and many types of electrical motors, generators and solenoids.

The heads are on long arms that go back to a powerful voice coil that allows extremely fast and accurate placement of the head. There is one head for each platter surface. If a drive has three platters, there are six heads, one on top and one on bottom of each of the platters.

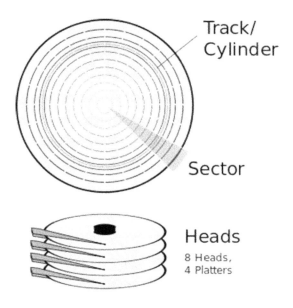

Track/
Cylinder

Sector

Heads
8 Heads,
4 Platters

Platters are divided into concentric rings called tracks. The tracks are further divided into sections called sectors. Each sector contains approximately 512 bytes of user data (this can be 1024, 2048 or 4096 bytes on some hard drives). Alongside this user data are other pieces of data for use by the hard drive such as the Preamble (used to ensure accurate data writing), Data Access Mark (the dividing line between Preamble and the User data), the CRC & ECC fields (used to ensure the data read is accurate), and various gaps to allow for the drive to finish reading sections during the time allowed. Generically these sections are divided into three areas of the sector; the header, data, and ECC areas.

A logical grouping of tracks on the hard drive platters used in addressing is called a cylinder. This cylinder consists of a track on the drive, and all the tracks perfectly above and below it. If a hard drive contains three platters and each platter has ten tracks, track five on each platter surface (top and bottom off each platter, or six total surfaces) is considered cylinder five.

Internally finding an area on the hard drive is done by the Physical Block Address (PBA). This address is derived from the Cylinder Head Sector (CHS) address. This change of address allows the hard drive to mark a sector as bad and remap the PBA to a new CHS. For example if PBA 123456 pointed to C5:H2:S8 (cylinder 5, head 2 and sector 8) and it was physically bad then the hard drive could remap PBA 123456 to C5:H4:S1 and requests for PBA 123456 would still function as intended. The change in location would be completely transparent.

External access to this address scheme is done by Logical Block Address (LBA). The reason for the LBA is that the standards used for hard drive addressing by computers do not allow for the massive size of today's hard drives so an alternate method of addressing had to be used.

LBA -> PBA -> CHS

No hard drive ever manufactured is perfect. Every platter ever made has sectors that do not record data correctly or at all, these are called bad sectors. On really old hard drives these bad sectors were actually printed on the drive label or written by hand on the drive. Those days are long gone as there are far too many sectors on a modern hard drive so that even if one tenth of one percent of the sectors are bad you could not possibly write that many sectors on the drive label.

We still mark bad sectors on the platters but now it is done inside the drive electronically. If your drive should develop a bad sector you can in theory add that to the bad sector map (the map is where the drive stores all the locations of the bad sectors) which will cause the drive to avoid using that sector from now on. Drives have the ability to add data to the bad sector table automatically when it detects that one has failed. Sometimes however this feature does not work as intended, or comes too late; that's when we need a helping hand.

Software such as SpinRite can not only test the drive for bad sectors and mark them as bad, but will attempt to recover data off of the bad sectors and move it to a new location on the hard drive. SpinRite is $90, available from www.grc.com and is the only software I know of that really does an excellent job at this. I will warn you that the process can be excruciatingly slow as it tries to read the sector many times to get your data back.

SpinRite works with virtually any file system and operating system because it boots to a DOS boot disc to run and is therefore OS and file system independent.

Here are some amazing facts about hard drives:

Modern hard drives can spin so fast that the outer edge of the platters are moving over 170MPH.

According to an article by Bill Hammack, hard drive platters are so smooth that if you enlarged the platter to the size of a football field the average bump would only be 3/100ths of an inch high.

The average height of the head above the platter is about 10 nanometers, or 10 billionths of a meter. In comparison a human hair ranges from 80,000-100,000 nanometers thick.

To illustrate what is happening inside a hard drive on a scale you can relate to, think of an eighteen wheeler (the hard drive head) driving down a road (the platter) at 145,000 MPH with the front bumper hovering approximately one tenth the thickness of a sheet of paper off the ground (height of the head above the platter).

If the tiniest speck of dust (about .5 Micrometers or 500 nanometers) lands on the platters it would be as if that eighteen wheeler above hit a fifteen inch high rock at full speed. The result of this impact would not be a pretty picture.

2.2.2 Flash Storage (USB/SSD/Devices)

Flash storage encompasses pretty much everything without moving parts. These include SSD (Solid State Drives, the replacement for hard drives), USB drives (sometimes called thumb drives or just flash drives), memory cards (such as SD/MicroSD/CF/Memory Stick Pro) and more. Most media players, cell phones, tablets and cameras have some form of flash storage.

Flash storage is made up of memory consisting of transistors called cells. These are arranged into Single-Level Cells (SLCs) or Multi-Level Cells (MLCs). Each level can store one bit so in an SLC there is one bit per cell while in a triple-level MLC there are three bits stored per cell.

Flash memory has a finite number of times it can be written to. This is called a P/E (program/erase) cycle. An example of a common lifecycle is up to one million P/E cycles. Because of this limitation drives include software to do Wear Leveling (a process used to evenly distribute writes to all sectors of the drive. In addition, erasing this type of memory can take a long time (comparatively) and so TRIM was developed to deal with this issue.

TRIM is a command that will take the delete command from the operating system and instruct the drive not to preserve the data in those cells any more. This makes those cells available for not only new files from the OS directly, but through wear leveling as well.

2.2.3 Optical discs (CD/DVD/BD)

Optical discs are discs where data is written to and read from using a laser. Common optical media includes Compact Discs (CDs), Digital Versatile Discs (DVDs) and Blu-Ray Discs (BDs).

There are two basic types of media used in optical drives: glass mastered and writable.

Glass mastered discs are created in large factories and mass produced. These discs typically last far longer than writable discs and are far cheaper to manufacture in bulk.

These types of discs have physical pits and lands representing the zeros and ones used to store the digital data on the disc. The ones and zeros are read by reading the changes in states from a land to a pit. This means if it is reading a pit and the next piece of data is another pit, there is no change and therefore a zero is read. If however the pit changes to a land, that change represents a one. The same holds true for land land and land pit readings respectively.

To create a mass produced disc they create the glass master using a device very similar to a traditional CD writer found in a personal computer except with a much higher powered laser. This creates a positive image, or a glass version of exactly what the finished product should be. Coatings on the disc are either directly burned away or are altered by the laser beam and later removed by a chemical developing process. Either way, physical lands and pits are the result of the process.

Next the glass master is used to press a negative image into a metal disc. Many of these discs are made as they tend to wear out with repeated uses. This metal negative image disc is then moved over to the presses.

Polycarbonate plastic pellets are melted into a machine which has molds shaped like the final discs. Once the discs are molded and cooled they are coated with a metallic reflective material, cured by using UV light and then pressed with the negative metal disc which creates a positive plastic disc. Finally this disc is coated with a lacquer to protect the disc and then it is sent to packaging.

Blu-Ray discs go one step further and coat the disc with a very durable coating which is far less likely to scratch than CDs or DVDs. It certainly does not mean they will not scratch, just that they put up with abuse far better.

Depending on who you ask, and depending on how you store them, commercial mass produced discs like this should last many years, up to forty some manufacturer's claim. They are affected by humidity, heat and abrasion which can substantially shorten their useful lives. Leaving them in your car through summer is a really bad idea.

An interesting note is that the part of the disc that contains the data is actually very close to the label side of the disc. This means that scratches or even ink from permanent markers could easily cause issues on that side. Scratches to the other side can actually be repaired by refilling the scratches with a lacquer or light polishing.

Writable discs are a little different as they are written in your computer.

The writable disc from its factory is a polycarbonate plastic disc filled with a dye that changes color when exposed to light. The computer drive has two laser modes, low power which is used for reading and high power which is used to write. When the high power laser hits the photosensitive dye in the disc it changes colors, altering the reflectiveness of that bit on the disc. As the read laser examines the disc it reads the disc just like a standard glass master pressed disc looking for the change from one bit to the next and assigning no change as a zero and a change as a one.

Writable discs are more susceptible to problems from light and heat than are the glass pressed ones since they contain a photosensitive dye. Manufacturers list the life of a writable disc at between 20 and 100 years depending on the quality of the components used in its manufacture. Actual results are likely to be far lower for any disc not kept in perfect conditions such as low temperatures, low humidity, total darkness and with no handling.

Rewritable discs are exactly like writable discs but use a special metal alloy in place of the dye layer. This has the advantage of allowing the metal to change state from amorphous to crystalline and back which alters its reflectivity back and forth. The problem is that this change does not alter the reflectivity nearly as much as a standard writable disc which means older drives may not be able to read rewritable discs.

Note that all optical drives can read commercially pressed media and the vast majority can read the vast majority of burn once media (CD-R, DVD-R, DVD+R, BD-R) but due to the reduced reflectivity of re-writable media (CD-RW, DVD-RW, DVD+RW, BD-RE) many drives cannot read these unless they are designed to create the discs themselves. This means that if you put a movie onto a DVD-RW disc, your home DVD player connected to your TV probably will not be able to read it.

The data structure on CDs is very similar to the data structure on hard drives. Sectors are 2,352 bytes long and contain nothing but audio on audio CDs and for CD-ROMs (the data version of CDs) contains the following:

Mode1: 12 Sync : 2 Address : 1 Mode : 2,048 Data : 4 Error detection : 8 Reserved : Error correction

Mode2: 12 Sync : 3 Address : 1 Mode : 2,336 Data

CD-ROM drives use a laser in the 780nm spectrum while DVD uses 650nm and Blu-Ray uses 405nm.

DVDs come in single layer (just like CDs) and dual layer versions. Dual layers are achieved by stacking two layers with the top most (closest to the laser) semi-transparent. The lower layer is read by shifting the focus of the laser beam to the second layer allowing light to pass through the upper layer and reflect primarily off the lower layer. In addition to this change in focus, the data bits on the lower layer are shifted so that the data bits do not stop and start at the same point as the bits on the upper layer. DVDs can hold approximately 4.7GB for a single layer and 8.5GB for a dual layer.

Blu-Ray discs are similar in structure to both DVD and CD but can contain even more data, roughly 25GB per layer. Currently 50GB dual layer discs are common and 128GB quad layer discs have been demonstrated. As of 2015 the Blu-Ray Alliance announced that two new formats holding 66GB on dual layers and 100GB on triple layer discs will be new standards for the higher definition 4K TVs with high dynamic range (UHD Premium sets).

There are mini versions of CDs, DVDs and BDs but it is unlikely you will run into them frequently if at all. These mini versions use basically the same structure with just less capacity.

2.3 File systems

The sections that follow on file systems are by no means exhaustive or overly technical. They are not meant to be. The reason I included them is that certain pieces of information about file systems such as FAT systems usually contain two file allocation tables and can be important if one of them becomes corrupt. Some utilities will allow you to switch to the second table which can help you regain your data.

2.3.1 FAT

The FAT file system (File Allocation Table, types 0x0B and 0x0C) was originally designed in 1977 for floppy disks. Through the years it has grown through its original 8bit incarnation and versions in 12bit, 16bits and finally a 32bit version. The latest version is still used today on many devices such as flash storage in cameras and USB flash drives.

It is very unlikely that you will encounter anything in the FAT file system before FAT32 since it was natively supported in Windows starting with Windows 2000.

FAT32 allows for a 2TB partition with a sector size of 512 bites and a 16TB partition with a sector size of 4096. Even with these large partition sizes a problem occurs with the maximum file size of 4GB which is easily exceeded by today's video files and even Outlook PST (mail storage) files.

The FAT file system is divided into four logical areas; the reserved region, the FAT region, the root directory region and the data region.

The reserved region is at the beginning of the drive and contains the boot sector (can be sector 0 only or 0 through 2) and other generic file system information. There is often a backup boot sector (sectors 6-8) as well.

The FAT region contains one, or more often, two copies of the file allocation table. These tables have the physical addresses of all the files and directories stored in the data region. The second copy of the tables is almost never used however it is possible to access it using some diagnostic software.

The root directory region is a legacy section used by FAT12 and FAT16 only, it is not used in FAT32.

The data region is where the actual files and folders are stored.

The two biggest problems with the FAT file system other than not being able to handle files larger than 4GB are fragmentation and slack.

Fragmentation is when a file of say ten clusters (the smallest area addressable by the files system is a cluster) is written to the disk, then another file is written after it. The ten cluster file is then deleted and a fifteen cluster file is written. This causes ten of the fifteen new clusters of data to be written in the void left by the previously deleted ten cluster file, and then the remaining five clusters will be written after the next file. This breaking apart of a file to fit it into the available space is called fragmentation.

To solve the problem many aftermarket disk defragmenters have been developed through the years. In addition Windows eventually put in its own defragmentation program. Newer versions of Windows can even defragment the drive automatically.

Keep fragmentation in mind as the file you are recovering may not be in one contiguous block but could instead be in many sections spread all over the drive. This becomes important when using a disk sector editor to view the information sector by sector.

Slack occurs because data can only be written in clusters. If you have a cluster size of 64k and you write a 65k file it consumes two clusters of space or 128K, the remaining 63K of the second cluster is wasted. Multiply this out to hundreds of thousands of files or more on the drive and you can have a serious problem with wasted space.

It is important to take slack into consideration when recovering as there may be data in a sector that does not belong to the file being recovered. Say for example a 64k cluster was completely in use with file ABC123.DEF but then that file was deleted and the cluster now only is using the first 1k of file GHI456.JKL. Strange things can happen.

2.3.2 NTFS

NTFS (New Technology File System) was introduced in 1993 by Microsoft as a replacement for FAT. NTFS is faster, more efficient and includes many new features to improve security and reliability. Modern versions include support for file compression, disk quotas, encryption, redundant master file table data, and security descriptors.

According to Microsoft, NTFS supports maximum file size and maximum disk size of 18,446,744,073,709,551,616 bytes or 16 Exabytes. To put that into perspective, the largest commercially available hard drive today is 8TB, NTFS can support up to 16,777,216TB. That might hold us a few years!

NTFS disks can be either basic or dynamic. Basic disks are just that, basic. They are what typical computers use and contain partitions and logical drives. These are limited to a maximum of four partitions using MBR or 128 using GPT (MBR and GPT are discussed later).

Dynamic disks are like basic disks but with many enhanced features such as the ability to create software based RAID (see the section on RAID drives later in the book for a detailed definition) and for partitions to span across multiple hard drives.

Dynamic disks use a database stored on the drive to store configuration information about the drive. This database is located in the last 1MB on MBR partitions and in a hidden 1MB partition on GPT partitions and include self repairing duplicate databases. This database design allows you to have a virtually unlimited number of volumes on a dynamic drive although Microsoft recommends limiting it to 32.

A common error you see when an NTFS partition can not be booted is a bad or missing Ntldlr.dll. This is the file that is responsible for starting the file system, reading the boot.ini and starting the boot process to your operating system. When you see an error like this it typically means that you have either selected the incorrect boot device (you would be amazed how often this happens) or the boot sector of the hard drive is damaged.

An important part of NTFS for file recovery is the Volume Shadow Copy service or VSS. This service keeps previous versions of files on the drive. Utilities such as Shadow Explorer (www.shadowexplorer.com Windows 7/8) can make use of these to restore otherwise deleted, damaged or encrypted files. I really liked Shadow Explorer because it had a portable version I could simply use from my flash drive but it does not seem to work well under Windows 10.

Z-VSScopy (from www.z-dbackup.com) is another free program (for personal use) for dealing with shadow copies and it works with Windows XP through 10 and even on Windows Server up to 2012R2 (albeit as a 14 day trial on server OSs).

NTFS drives can be read on all modern Windows versions as well as on Mac and Linux machines with additional aftermarket plugins.

You have seen several mentions of MBR and GPT so let's take a minute to see what those actually are.

MBR or Master Boot Record has been a standard in operating systems since the early 1980s around the time of DOS 2.0. The MBR is basically a section of the disk where it stores data about the layout of partitions and other information required to boot.

Since it is so old there are several restrictions, the most important of which is that you cannot have a volume larger than 2TB in size. This has only become an issue in the last few years where it is not at all uncommon to see 4TB and larger hard drives.

Many utilities can repair a problem with the MBR. Back in the old days we would use the DOS command "FDISK /MBR" to repair the boot sector when it was corrupted and you can do pretty much the same today. Use the disc or USB drive that came with your computer, boot to your computer's recovery partition, or boot to the recovery media you made when you got your computer and open the recovery command prompt. Once there you can use the command "BOOTREC /FIXMBR" to do the same thing as the old command.

The replacement for MBR is called GPT which is the Globally unique identifier Partition Table. This type of partition scheme allows for drives over 8ZB or zettabytes. That translates out to one billion terabytes. That's right, the 1TB hard drive in your computer you bought recently? One billion of those hard drives makes 1ZB.

One issue you may have using this technology is that if you want to boot to a large drive, for example a 4TB drive, and you are running Windows or MacOS, then you need to have a computer with UEFI BIOS. Non-UEFI BIOS can certainly use a GPT drive of 4TB but it just cannot boot to it.

So what is a UEFI BIOS?

The BIOS (Basic Input Output System) is the code that is embedded in the motherboard of your computer that allows the machine to start working. It also contains code that allows you to configure options such as what device should be the boot device, turning on and off pieces of hardware like your sound card, etc. This is the code that provides the infrastructure that allows an operating system to boot on the computer. Without it, no disk or device would be able to operate or boot at all.

UEFI (Unified Extensible Firmware Interface) is the more modern replacement for the BIOS and adds new options such as a modular design that is CPU independent. This means they do not have to write new code for each new CPU and can use modules to support different hardware configurations. In some cases UEFI also supports remote diagnostics even if your computer will not boot to the operating system. And of course it supports larger drives.

Typically UEFI is backwards compatible with BIOS and although it replaces the BIOS and many people call it the UEFI BIOS, its correct name is simply UEFI.

2.3.3 HFS+

Apple computers, commonly called Macs since the first Macintosh model computer was released by Apple in January 1984 currently use a file system called HFS+ (Hierarchical File System plus). It was introduced in January 1998 with MacOS 8.1 and continues today with MacOS 10.11 El Capitan and even MacOS Sierra.

Originally HFS+ volumes were placed inside a HFS volume to provide support for Macs that did not have HFS+ support in their BIOS code. Since this was for users of operating systems prior to MacOS 8.1 it is unlikely you would run into this but I did want to point it out just in case someone pulls a computer out of their attic.

HFS+ volumes are divided into sectors of 512 bytes and then these sectors are grouped into allocation blocks. Each allocation block can contain one or more sectors. The current version of HFS+ can access roughly four billion allocation units or about eight exebytes.

The layout of the file system starts with the first two sectors, 0 and 1. These are the HFS boot blocks.

The next sector is sector 2 and is the Volume Header where data such as allocation block size and location of other data files are stored.

Several files contain file system data starting with the Allocation File which lists all allocation blocks on the drive along with a 0 if the block is available/empty or a 1 if it is currently in use. This file could be stored anywhere on the drive and may not be a single contiguous file.

The Catalog File contains the location information for every file and directory on the volume along with other file related information. This is basically a large database file.

The drive also contains the Extents Overflow, Attributes and Startup files which are normally not relevant to data recovery.

Most of the technicians I know use Windows PC for most of their work out of necessity. This means that it would be very nice if their Windows based PCs could read and/or write to HFS+ drives. There are several ways to accomplish this.

The first method of accessing a HFS+ drive on a Windows machine is to use the free HFSExplorer software (www.catacombae.org). I know people who swear by this software however I have not had good luck with it. I mention it here simply because of the number of people I hear have success with it.

Another option is Paragon HFS+ for Windows (www.paragon-software.com). Unfortunately it is not free but for only $20 you can have the Mac drive mounted just like any Windows drive and use it fully. Anything you can do with a Windows drive, you can do with this software and a Mac drive. Be sure you try the trial first to make sure it works for you, and make sure you have backups of your PC since this is a file system driver. If something goes wrong it can stop your machine from booting.

Lastly is the option I hear the best about (actually, I hear the least bad, how is that?), Macdrive (www.mediafour.com). This is a little more expensive than Paragon's HFS+ at $50 for the standard version but has quite a few more tricks up its sleeve such as repair utilities that work on HFS+.

Being able to read and write to Mac drives has come in very handy for me over the years and this software has proven to be well worth the money.

2.3.4 EXT

The ext file system has been through a lot of revisions starting in 1992 as the first file system built specifically for Linux.

The current version of ext is ext4 and supports drives up to 1EB or exebyte in size. That is roughly a million terabytes. It supports individual files of 16TB in size.

Ext4 is very efficient, storing up to 128MB of information in a single contiguous section called an extent. These extents help reduce fragmentation and also reduce slack as they are made up of small 4k blocks.

This file system is a hierarchical file system both in the way the user interacts with it (files in folders in drives) but also in the way it stores data. Data is stored in blocks which are organized into extents, these are then grouped into a maximum of four extents per file making up an inode. Should a file require more than an inode (more than a 512MB file) then the rest of the file is stored in a tree.

Should you need to, www.paragon-software.com offers drivers for both Windows and MacOS to read and write Linux ext2/3/4 file systems. Yes, you can do file recovery with Windows and MacOS tools using these drivers. No, the drivers are not free.

As of this writing I have found no reliable and stable free filesystem drivers for ext on Windows or MacOS. Then again, you can just do the recovery on a Linux computer and not worry about it!

2.3.5 Optical formats

Optical disc formats are very colorful, no really! CD formats for example are denoted by the color of the book that contained the specifications. These books define the physical characteristics of the disc itself (red book) and the physical layout of data on the disc.

Red Book is the specification released in 1980 to cover audio CDs or CD-DA (Compact Disc-Digital Audio). It is also defines the physical standards of the disc which all subsequent book use.

Yellow Book released in 1988 defined CDROMs (Compact Disc Read Only Memory) which of course held all our data and for years was the standard way to distribute computer software. Yellow book had two modes, mode 1 and mode 2.

Mode 1 stores data in a 2,352 byte block which allowed for 2048 bytes of data and a further 280 bytes used for error correction of the data. This mode is used by virtually all typical data CDs.

Data in mode 1 is stored as follows: 12 bytes of sync data, 3 bytes of address data, one byte to designate the mode (0x01), 2048 bytes of data, 4 bytes for error detection, 8 bytes reserved and 276 bytes for error correction.

Mode 2 is virtually the same as mode 1 except there is no error correction and it uses 2336 byte data blocks.

Data in mode 2 is stored as follows: 12 bytes of sync data, 3 bytes of address data, one byte to designate the mode (0x02), and 2336 bytes of data.

Orange Book defined all the CDR (Compact Disc Recordable), CDRW (Compact Disc ReWritable) and magneto optical formats such as Minidisc. This was released in 1990.

Beige Book in 1992 defined the photo CD.

White Book from 1993 was the specification for VCD (Video Compact Disc) which was an attempt at putting movies on CDs which failed pretty miserably.

Scarlet Book gave us SACD (Super Audio Compact Disc) in 1999. While SACD never really gained traction it is still available today and assuming you have a good audio system and a SACD player (it requires a specific type of player) still sounds amazing.

There are even more books such as green, purple and blue for things you will probably never see.

For data discs you have the book such as yellow book and then the file system such as ISO9660, Joliet or HFS.

ISO9660 is a file system that allows virtually any computer to read a disc. It limits the file names to eight characters with a further three character extension such as abcdefgh.abc. This was extended by Microsoft with Joliet which allows for Unicode characters and 64 character filenames.

Some discs for Macintosh computers were done in HFS format just like their hard drives.

2.3.6 APFS

With the arrival of Apple's new operating system, Sierra, a new file system has arrived. This new system is called the Apple File System or APFS for short. This is exciting because it is the first new file system released by Apple in eighteen years and promises some really nice new features.

While APFS is included in Sierra it is considered to still be in beta (a testing phase not meant for general use). They say it should be ready for prime time somewhere in 2017 so it is unlikely you will see many of these in need of recovery any time soon.

Unlike other file systems, this one was built to take advantage of the extremely fast flash and SSD storage in use today.

Clones (not a hard drive clone as we are discussing it, just a name for a feature) provide Windows shadow copy like functionality with a twist. Instead of just keeping multiple copies of a file it keeps the original and then "difference" files which only contain the changes. This makes storing multiple versions of a file take up less space and make the copying process much faster.

APFS provides three different levels of encryption built right into the file system. This includes not encrypted, one key for everything encryption, and a separate key for each file and another for the metadata.

You can create snapshots which basically takes an image of your file system and write protects it so nothing can alter it. This is fantastic for backups or to help prevent mass encryption cryptolocker programs.

To make it simple, the new APFS should be faster, more reliable and less likely to lose data even when a drive suffers a failure such as a bad sector.

Unfortunately since this is so new and still in beta there is very little actual data on it.

Part 3: Deleted/Corrupted file recovery

So what causes deleted or corrupt files?

The first thing of course is that the user just accidently deleted the file. This could be they hit the delete key while the file was highlighted and that moved the file into the recycle bin or they might have grabbed a bunch of files and dragged them to the shredder, with one they didn't intend.

It could also be that the file was "overwritten" by saving a new file with the same filename as the old file.

Corruption could be from the computer losing power as the file was being written to, or sometimes simply because the file was in use. It could also be that you have a bad sector on the hard drive or a bad piece of memory. In some cases an overheating computer can cause file corruption.

Both deleted and corrupt files could be caused by failing hardware so it is important when in doubt of the cause that you remove the storage media from the user's computer and put it in a bench machine to run tests and recovery whenever possible.

Whatever the cause files that are deleted or corrupt are generally the mainstay of data recovery technicians.

3.1 Windows PCs

The most common problem on Windows PCs is simple file deletion. You meant to delete file XXX but instead deleted file YYY, oops.

Of course the first thing you should do is look in the recycle bin, you know, that thing that looks like a trash can on your desktop. It isn't there? Let's fix that first.

On Windows Vista/7/8 right click on the desktop and select Personalize. Select Change desktop icons near the top left. A box will pop up with settings for what icons show on the desktop, make sure that recycle bin has a check mark next to it.

On Windows 10 right click on the desktop and select Personalize. Select Themes on the left side and then Desktop icon settings on the right. A box will pop up with settings for what icons show on the desktop, make sure that recycle bin has a check mark next to it.

Now that we have a recycle bin, let's double click on it and see what is inside.

If the file you want to restore is there, right click on it and select Restore. Windows will put the file back where it was originally when you deleted it.

Assuming that did not solve your problem (the file was not there) then we need to go a little further and use some recovery software.

I always try to work with a clone of the original disk (see the section earlier in the book about "Making a backup or clone") when possible. Failing that, I remove the disk from the machine and connect it to my machine (see the section earlier in the book on "Things you may need" for ways to attach a drive to another computer). If the file is not in the recycle bin, the last resort (that I almost never use) is to work on the machine with the deleted file by using a boot CD or USB drive (Bootable discs and USB drives are discussed in the earlier section on "Making a backup or clone").

The first program I typically try is called Recuva and is available for free from www.piriform.com. They also have a professional version for about $25 with more advanced recovery features and support but it is surprising how well the free version works.

Once Recuva is downloaded and installed (Not on the machine with the deleted files as this could overwrite where the file used to be and ruin any chance of recovery), running it starts the wizard. I use a USB cradle attached to a bench machine with Recuva installed on the bench machine.

I typically select all files, however you can select a specific type if you are looking for just one specific type of file.

Here you can speed up the search if you know exactly where the file was when it was deleted, or you can select "I'm not sure" which will search all your hard drives. Since I attach the customer's drive to my bench machine I select the "In a specific location" selection and use the browse button to select the drive I am working with.

Note the checkbox for a deep scan. I normally do a deep scan on all customer's drives simply because if it was an easy fix they would not have brought it to me. Additionally I do this on a bench machine so I can be working on another project while this is taking an hour or more to scan.

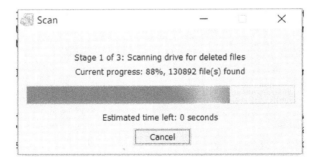

The progress indicator will start moving while it scans.

Once the scan is finished Recuva presents you with a list of files it found. If you see the one you want simply put a check mark in the box to the left of the filename (or check the box at the very top left to recover all the files it found) and then click the Recover button in the bottom right.

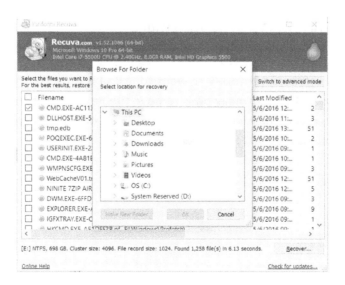

Recuva asks you where you want to put the recovered files. I usually create a new folder just for this and recover the files into that new folder.

Once the recovery is complete Recuva will tell you how many files were fully and partially recovered. A partially recovered document may contain vital information that is usable while a partially recovered image may not even be viewable.

If even a deep scan with Recuva did not get your file back then I will try Partition Guru (www.eassos.com). They have a free version with a lot of limitations but the professional version at $70 is a real bargain for all the capabilities it has and how well it works.

In order to use this software you do NOT want to install it on the computer that you are recovering data from. What I normally do is remove the hard drive from the computer and connect it to another computer via USB. Once that drive is visible in Windows I launch Partition Guru (which I will call PG from now on).

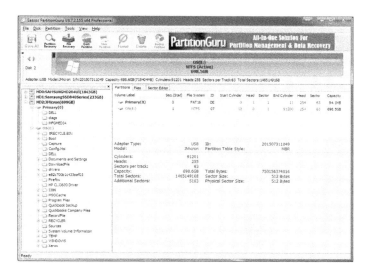

On the left side I select the drive I will be working on. In my case since I am using a USB adapter with a JMicron chipset in it that is how it shows up. The other two drives above the JMicron are the hard drives in the computer I am connecting this to.

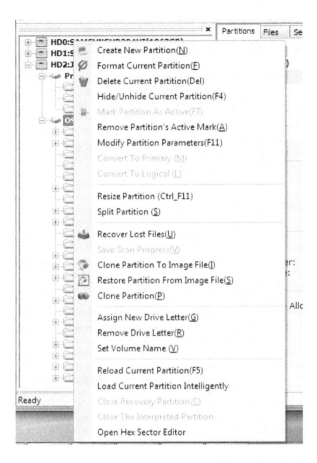

Once the drive you want to work on is selected on the left, right click on it and you will get a pop up menu listing a bunch of options. We want to select Recover Lost Files(U).

The Recover files dialog box pops up now and you can select the recovery type. I normally select Complete Recovery to make sure it shows me everything possible.

After clicking Start the screen changes and it starts searching. You can see here the progress it is making and how many files it has found so far.

Once the scan is complete (be patient, this can take a while) you will see over on the left it has put files into categories including Document Files, Photo Files and several other types. If it can identify the file type, then it sticks them in the appropriate list. Clicking on the plus sign on the left of each type opens it up to show you all the files in that type. You can select one or more files and then right click to bring up a menu.

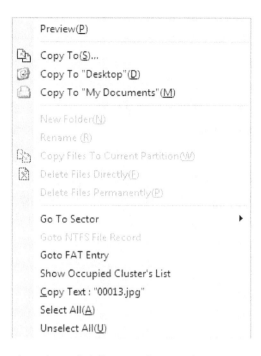

From this menu you can do a lot of different things, the most obvious is the three Copy commands allowing you to copy the recovered file to a location of your choice.

PG now copies the file to the location you specified and you are done.

If you are forced to work on the computer where the files were deleted instead of working with a clone or at least removing the hard drive and attaching it to another computer, you can use the UBCD we discussed earlier and run Parted Magic, and then run TestDisk from there. See the later section on Linux file recovery for instructions on using these utilities.

3.2 Apple PCs

Recovering files from a Mac is just like recovering files from a Windows PC albeit with different tools. Of course you need to remember that you should be working with a bit clone when possible or at the very least not installing the tools to do the recovery onto the same hard drive you are recovering data from.

Basic and even some advanced recovery can be done with EaseUS Data Recovery (www.easeus.com) for free. They also have a pro version that provides upgrades and support as well as allows you to recover data when the operating system will not start for whatever reason.

Once you download and install EaseUS Data Recovery (EDR from here on out) you can run it and select the type or types of files you are looking for. If you are unsure or want to see everything then you can select the checkbox for All types and click on Next.

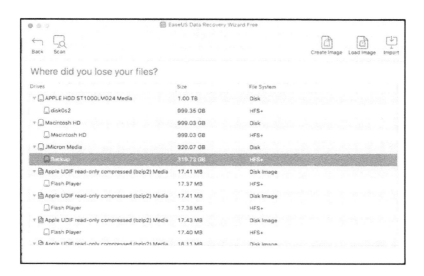

On the next screen you can select the drive or partition that had the data on it you need to recover by clicking on it and then clicking on Scan near the top left.

EDR will start the scan process and display the number of files found, along with the estimated time remaining to search the drive.

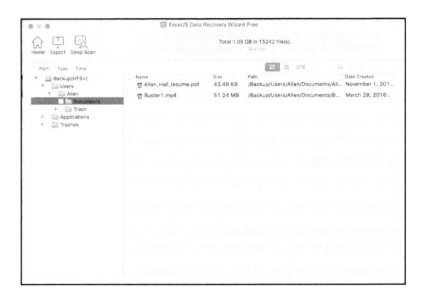

Once the scan is complete you can drill down on the left side to see the files it found in those areas over on the right. In this example there are two files that I deleted, a PDF and a video file, which are displayed on the right with checkboxes next to the filenames. Note the Deep Scan button that has appeared up near the top left. This Deep Scan button is in case you do not see the file you are trying to recover and causes the software to look harder for more files. This Deep Scan can take quite a while and may show you files that can only be partially recovered.

Once the files you want to recover are checked, the grayed out Recover button near the top center turns blue and you can click on it.

The previous screen displays where you can recover the files to. Remember to never recover the files to the same drive you are recovering from or it may start to overwrite some of the data with the recovered files. To clear this up a little, if you are recovering ten files when you recover the first file it may write that file over the space marked as empty for the fourth file so when it is time to recover that file the data is lost.

3.3 Linux PCs

On Linux I use TestDisk to recover files. It is also an excellent solution for Windows recovery if you have to boot from a CD on the customer's PC.

Insert the UBCD disc we discussed earlier and boot from it.

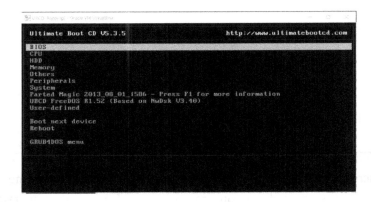

Select Parted Magic from the menu of options.

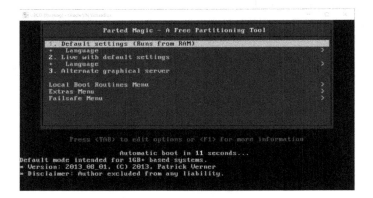

You can just press enter to accept the default settings.

You will see a lot of text scrolling on the screen as the software loads.

After it boots UBCD will ask for your time zone.

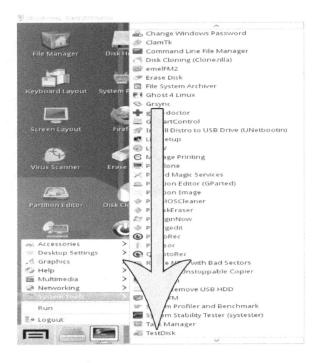

Once in Parted Magic off the UBCD disc, select the menu from the bottom left, then select system tools and near the bottom of the list is TestDisk.

If I boot from CD or DVD I select No Log from the first menu since you cannot write to CD/DVD. If booting from USB then I will select Create so that it will make a log I can use later for diagnostics if something does not go as well as I had hoped.

TestDisk will then show you a list of drives available for use allowing you to select the one you want to work with. Once you have it selected hit enter to proceed.

Next you need to select your partition type. When working on Windows this will normally be the top choice, Intel. TestDisk attempts to auto detect the correct partition type so the odds are it will be highlighted already for you.

On the next menu select Advanced.

TestDisk now shows you the partitions available to work on. Your drive may have one, two or more partitions. Generally speaking, and if you do not know which partition is which, I suggest you start with the largest one as that is the one most likely to have your data on it. Highlight the partition you want to work on and then select Undelete down at the bottom center.

Here is a list of the deleted files that TestDisk has found. If there are many files (most likely there will be a lot) you can use the ":" key to select the ones you want to recover. Once you have everything you want selected simply press "C" (the capital letter C) to copy the files to another drive (copying to the drive you are recovering from can cause you to lose data).

```
TestDisk 7.0, Data Recovery Utility, April 2015

Please select a destination where ./readme.txt will be copied.
Keys: Arrow keys to select another directory
      C when the destination is correct
      Q to quit
Directory /root
>drwxr-xr-x     0     0      360 10-May-2016 20:09 .
 drwxr-xr-x     0     0      240 10-May-2016 15:07 ..
 drwxr-xr-x     0     0      313 13-Jun-2013 14:51 Desktop
 drwxr-xr-x     0     0       40 10-May-2016 15:07 Documents
 drwxr-xr-x     0     0       40 10-May-2016 15:07 Downloads
 drwxr-xr-x     0     0       40 10-May-2016 15:07 Music
 drwxr-xr-x     0     0       40 10-May-2016 15:07 Pictures
 drwxr-xr-x     0     0       40 10-May-2016 15:07 Public
 drwxr-xr-x     0     0       40 10-May-2016 15:07 Templates
 drwxr-xr-x     0     0       40 10-May-2016 15:07 Videos
 drwxr-xr-x  1001  1001       80 24-May-2015 01:41 clamav
 drwxr-xr-x     0     0        3 23-May-2012 14:55 pyNeighborhood
 lrwxrwxrwx     0     0        6 28-Oct-2012 08:49 Media
 -rw-r--r--     0     0      804 23-Jan-2011 08:10 readme.txt
```

Select where you want the data saved (they call it copy instead of recover to or save to).

You're done!

3.4 Removable media

Removable media recovery is exactly the same as recovery from PCs. There are however some things to watch out for.

When dealing with cards or USB drives be sure to inspect the contacts on the connectors before you plug it in. These contacts not only can get covered with gunk and scratched up but can have the gold colored coatings actually peel off.

If the contacts are dirty use alcohol to clean them. While Vodka may work well too (not really, but it can be more fun!), I try to use 90% isopropyl alcohol which is usually available from the large department stores as well as most pharmacies. The higher the percentage of alcohol the better as it will tend to evaporate leaving less residue. If you have an electronics store nearby they also make a contact cleaner which is even better than alcohol but not nearly as readily available.

Another trick is to use the eraser on a pencil (assuming you still have pencils laying around, and they need to be soft erasers, not ones hard from being left in the drawer for years). This works extremely well at removing almost anything including stubborn material. Be sure to get all the eraser pieces off the contact when you are done. Alcohol can be used to clean off anything remaining.

If the contact coating peels off you can attempt to glue it back down using superglue although the glue frequently coats the top of the connector making it difficult to get a connection. Scraping the top of the connector with a knife or razor blade once the glue dries can help solve this.

If you used alcohol, or the owner put the media through the washing machine, be sure to let everything dry completely before inserting it into a reader. A wet SD card can short out a card reader instantly, which brings me to my next piece of advice.

Never put a memory card or USB drive that you know has some kind of issue (lost data, unable to access, whatever) into your computer. If something shorts out, you certainly do not want it to be a part inside your laptop! That is easily solved by carrying an external USB card reader and a small external powered USB hub. Both of these devices are very inexpensive (I just bought a really nice USB3 card reader for about $15 off Amazon) and easy to throw away and replace if a customer's media fries it.

Note that I mentioned getting a powered USB hub. This is because if something happens and the USB device pulls too much current it will most likely destroy the AC adapter provided with the hub and not the power supply or motherboard in your computer.

If a device has been in water or in high enough humidity such as dew, it is a good idea to make sure the internals are dry before working on it. Even if the outside is dry, the interior may be wet. I have heard a lot of ideas including packing the device in a container full of white rice and then placing that on top of a water heater. While I am not sure that is really necessary it probably will work. I like to save all those desiccant bags I get packed in with stuff in zip lock bags and then when I need to dry something out I can shove the item in a baggie with a few of those desiccant bags, keeping the whole thing on top of the water heater for a couple days just to make sure.

Note that when I say I put something on top of the water heater I mean just that. I want the temperature to be slightly warm to help the liquid evaporate. Under no conditions would I recommend actually heating the drive/card. No ovens, no microwaves, no bonfires. Just no. Heating up the drive/card will more than likely cause more damage than it will do good.

There is almost nothing to gain from taking a USB drive or memory card apart. I have never seen a problem with a connection or something I could fix inside one of these. If you are feeling frisky and have time to waste however it can be fun just to rip them apart and see what they look like. Even if they were in water and you want to take them apart to help them dry you are more likely to cause some physical damage than you are to help the situation.

Part 4: Failed media recovery

Failed media means that something has physically failed. This could be scratches on your CD, a missing or defective head in your hard drive, a bad sector, or even moisture inside a flash drive.

Here we will talk about ways to get around the physical failure including everything up to replacing components to try and get it working again.

4.1 Diagnostics

Failed media can cause a wide range of issues from a single bad sector to a hard drive that will not power on or spin. Previously we talked about different types of hardware failures and some possible ways to recover data. Here we will expand on that.

If the drive will not power on, or will not spin, you have a couple of choices; board replacement or platter/head replacement, both covered later in the Failed Media Recovery section. Since those are already covered, let's work on the most common types of hardware issues; slow access and bad sectors.

Some media will over time develop areas that will not read at full speed. In fact some of these will read so slow you will not be sure if it is doing anything at all for quite some time. I worked on a customer's external hard drive one time that copied only a few percentages of the total data over an entire weekend. The data did transfer, eventually, but it took weeks.

When working with something like an external hard drive you may think disassembling the drive would yield better results, and sometimes it will. Be very careful as some external drives are not meant to be disassembled and may not have a standard SATA connection inside. This may require you to be able to do some pretty good soldering to get it working.

Another issue is that some of these external drives may have an encryption chip in the enclosure that is married to the particular drive. This means that even if the drive reads perfectly fine outside the enclosure, the data on that drive may be encrypted preventing you from using the data you copied.

I always try to copy the data from an external drive in the enclosure first. If that completely fails, or the customer gets impatient and demands faster results knowing the risks, then I may remove it carefully and try again.

Many types of media may also develop bad sectors which simply cannot be read, or are unreliable. Certain types of software such as SpinRite can read the disc over and over to eventually get a pretty good amount of data back. Unfortunately many of these programs no longer read modern file systems. On the other hand, cloning programs have filled this void nicely and programs such as HDClone will attempt several reads and vary the speed of those reads to do a remarkable job of data recovery.

When cloning bad media be sure that you are prepared for it to take a considerable amount of time. There is no way to predict how long. If a normal clone would take an hour with this media then a clone of damaged media could take from an hour to a week. I always try to do a clone on a normal machine first but if it seems like it will take a long time, I stop the clone and restart it on a bench machine that I can leave it running on for as long as it takes.

An interesting aside here is that if you intend on letting the clone go for a long time, you might want to make sure that the machine your clone is running on has a battery backup unit on it. It really stinks when you let a clone go for several days and then a power failure makes you do it all over again.

Once the clone is done it is possible that you could just start using the new media that you cloned the image over to. For example when cloning a hard drive that contained the operating system for a Windows PC it is possible that installing the clone into the PC and turning it on will result in a fully functional PC and you are done.

It is also possible that this will result in a machine that will not boot at all, or one that boots and works most of the time but randomly has issues. There is simply no telling. The first thing I like to do is look at the software I made the clone with and see if it tells me how many sectors it failed to copy. This is different from the number of sectors that it thinks are bad. If the number that failed to transfer is very low then I may try to boot the machine and see how it works. If the number is very high I most likely will not even try, I will just hook the new clone up to a PC and recover the user's data off the drive.

The reason is that there is no telling what data was on those sectors. If the machine seems to work and you give the PC back to the customer they may launch a certain program, visit a certain website or do some other specific task that requires a specific file, and boom!

If for whatever reason you cannot help but use a clone that has a high number of bad sectors and it does actually boot one thing you can do that may help is to run the System File Checker in Windows ("sfc /scannow" from an administrator's command prompt) or the repair utilities under Disk First Aid in MacOS. You Linux users don't really have to worry too much as the file system is checked automatically if there is an error, and on roughly every 30th boot even if there is no error detected.

Where the bad sectors were also plays an important part in what is recovered. If the sectors were right at the beginning, then it is likely that the operating system may not boot at all. If the sectors are near the end and the drive has a large amount of free space then it is possible that the damage was in an empty area and no files were harmed. In between could mean that the operating system is fine, but files and programs could be damaged.

4.2 Standard methods

When you think the media, such as a hard drive, has failed the very first thing you need to do is to reseat the cables on the device and the computer to make sure they have not come loose. You can also clean the connections by wiping them with alcohol and/or using a stiff nylon brush. Do not use a metal brush as this could actually remove the plating that makes the contacts and ruin the drive.

Next try it in a different computer. It could be something like a problematic cable or weak power supply in the original computer. For external hard drives that have a separate power supply, see if you can find a different power supply and test again. If you get the same results then it probably is not the power supply.

After eliminating the easy stuff the standard methods of failed media recovery are exactly the same as deleted file recovery; attempt a clone and do file recovery from there. It is amazing how often this works without going any further.

4.3 Brute force

There are times when you need to "persuade" the device to work when it just doesn't want to. This can be necessitated by a wide range of hardware failures most of which you cannot physically get to without taking a significant risk. Fortunately there are a few tricks.

Freeze it. Hard drives in particular can benefit from this as the reduction in temperatures tends to tighten things up. If you have a deep freeze use that and put the drive in the very bottom as heat rises. Leave the drive at least overnight and try it again in the morning.

Remember that if freezing the drive looks like it will work, work very quickly as the drive may start to get more problematic as it warms up. I have had this work an impressive number of times when a drive will not come up at all, sometimes when the computer does not see it at all, and sometimes when the drive just sits there and clicks. Make no mistake that this is a Hail Mary however.

This trick also works on USB drives occasionally for some of the same reasons, things tighten up. Although I cannot say for certain, I am guessing that connections get tighter and electrical connections are better, for a limited time. It has worked a time or two for me but I have to admit it is very rare. Since it doesn't cost me anything but time it never hurts to try.

If the hard drive will not spin up at all there is another method which may work but is to be considered a last ditch method. Hit it. Long ago it was common for the old MFM and RLL drives to have bearings that wore out and the drive would not spin up. We literally would apply power to the drive and slam it into the counter to make it start spinning.

While the bearings in today's hard drives do not really suffer from this it is still possible that something inside the drive has jammed and is preventing the platters from spinning up. The problem with this is there is a very high likelihood that if this works at all, it will work exactly one time and you better be ready to get the data off right this second as it could catastrophically fail at any moment.

If you are attempting to make a clone and are having a difficult time, you can try turning the drive to a different orientation and making another clone. Remarkably this actually can actually get you a better clone.

In other words, if you have the drive sitting on its bottom with the board down as it would normally sit and you get a large number of bad sectors. Try turning the drive upside down and cloning it again.

You can even try a third attempt with the drive on its side.

It is remarkable how often this can actually reduce the amount of read errors and make it substantially more likely you can get some kind of data off the drive.

I have heard that the magnets are weak and shifting the way the drive faces allows gravity to assist the magnet.

I have heard that the extra pull of gravity on a head that is too close/far from the platter can assist in the reading of the data.

Honestly I have no idea why, I just know it works sometimes. Give it a shot, what do you have to lose?

4.4 Board replacement

Occasionally the exterior electronic board on a drive fails, usually from an electrical surge or physical damage to a connector. This is popular to see after a storm or with people who like to try to work on their own computers. Often the drive will not spin up at all, or sometimes it will spin but not read or not be detected by the computer.

Occasionally you can get the drive to work with a cracked or partially broken connector by just carefully plugging it in with no tension on the cables at all. When that fails, or if the connector(s) are broken completely, it is time to think about a board replacement.

The trick to replacing the board is coming up with an identical and known good replacement board. It is not enough to have the same model drive, it needs to be exactly the same board. For example I had a dead Western Digital WD5000AAKS drive come in the other day which did not spin up at all. I found another WD5000AAKS from around the same time and tried that board in the failed drive, it did spin the drive up but the computer would not see it.

This did not surprise me as the boards were very close to the same but not exact. The shape was the same, the major components were in the same places, etc. The boards were ever so slightly different shades of green and they had minor marking differences. All it takes is one little change and it won't work.

I was fortunate in that a little more searching revealed another WD5000AAKS in another pile and the board was indeed identical in color and layout. Using that board not only spun up the dead drive but also made it readable in Windows. I was able to recover all of the customer's data just copying it off using the standard Windows copy command.

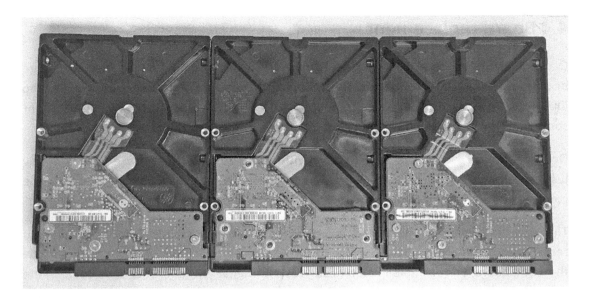

In the above image the first drive is the customer's dead drive. The center board was the first one I found that did make the drive spin up but was still unreadable, note the slight shade of green difference between it and the first one (if you are looking at the printed book note the shade of gray difference). The board on the far right was an exact match and worked flawlessly after being transplanted to the drive on the left.

One word of caution is that if the drive is seriously damaged, that damage may not just be to that external board. If the internal components are seriously damaged then plugging a known good board onto the drive could damage that good board. Never remove the board on a known working drive unless you are willing to throw that drive away as well.

I have had no luck sourcing these boards by themselves, however eBay has been an excellent source of drives for which donor parts can be removed. The trick is to have high resolution pictures of both sides of the drive, or be willing to take a chance. If the bottom of the drive is not pictured, often a quick message to the seller will solve that issue. Buying a complete drive from eBay or another source also has the benefit of allowing you to test the entire assembly as a unit and then you know if the board is good or not.

Replacing these is typically an easy task. In the pictured WD5000AAKS drives it is simply five torx headed screws and then lift the board up. There are no connectors and the little resistance you may feel is from the small foam pad stuck to the board which can sometimes also adhere to the drive case as well.

Simply remove the screws, lift the board, put on the new board, replace the screws, plug in the drive and test.

Newer drives may be more of a challenge. There is a firmware chip on the logic board that may have information that the drive requires to read the file system. This was once written only to the platters, and still often is, but many times it may be in the firmware and if that is the case replacing the board will not fix the problem.

One tech I know talked about finding the firmware chip and physically desoldering it off the old board and soldering it to the new board. While this may indeed work, it is not for the faint of heart as this level of soldering takes experience, practice, and the correct tools.

Any way it goes, keep in mind that this is very much a last ditch effort to recover data off an otherwise dead drive. Do not attempt to do this if you plan on sending the drive in for professional clean room recovery as you may make things worse. If you have nothing to lose, give it a shot, I have had it work wonderfully a few times.

4.5 Platter/Head replacement

When all else fails and you have no choice, you can open the drive and attempt to work on it. Without an actual real lab with a clean room, you are at the very least about 90% likely to accomplish nothing but wasting time and destroying the drive permanently. I have never had this actually do much of anything else.

There is a chance, a very small chance, less than the chance of winning the lottery probably, that you could get the data off the drive before it just completely crashed. This section will walk you through the disassembly and reassembly process assuming you want to try.

Please note that my disassembly and reassembly is targeted at providing adequate pictures and diagrams, not at actually recovering data so I certainly will not be in a clean room or observing the best practices to ensure data recovery.

If you want to try this at home and want to do every ridiculous thing you can think of to hope for any data recovery you need the cleanest part of your house. My recommendation would be to go into your bathroom, either close off any air conditioner ducts (and by that I mean seal them off with tape or magnetic covers, not just close the little vents), seal the cracks around the doors, run hot water for a while to steam the room, wait for the steam to go away and then clean everything you can (the steam will collect dust etc from the air, that will settle onto everything and then you can clean it all off) and be sure to wear non-powdered medical type gloves.

Yes, all of that is a little, ummmm, ridiculous, but if you are desperate enough to take a drive apart to get data back and cannot afford to send the drive in to a professional data recovery lab, then I think anything that might give you a one tenth of one percent better chance of getting the data back is worth it. Besides, then you will have a really clean bathroom!

Different manufacturers and different models of hard drives have different constructions so what follows is meant to lead you in the right direction, not as a blueprint for every drive out there. Some have different numbers of screws, different screw types, different covers, more or less heads/platters, etc. Use this guide to get you started.

To open a desktop hard drive you need to first remove the screws on the top of the drive. Most drives will have between five and nine screws which are usually something like a T8 screwdriver bit.

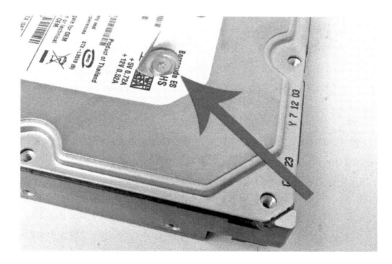

Once you remove the screws around the perimeter there is always one or two under the label. This allows the manufacturer to know if you opened the drive because you have to remove at least a portion of the label in order to remove the screw. You can find the location of the screws under the label by pressing on the label with your finger and feeling where the screws are. Once you find one, simply tear or cut that portion of the label away to gain access to the screw(s).

Now that you have all the screws removed you can take off the cover. This can be stuck pretty well so you may need to get a fingernail or the edge of a knife under a corner and gently pry the cover off. If it seems like the cover does not want to come off, make absolutely sure you have all the screws removed. There could be another one hiding under the label somewhere.

With the cover removed we can see the head and platters clearly. Since replacing the platters would result in losing your data the only things you can really do in here is to replace the heads or any circuit board inside the drive.

Since this drive does not have a circuit board, let's work on replacing the head assembly. First remove the screw behind the head assembly holding the large magnet in place. You will need to be careful removing this magnet as it is very powerful and once the field is broken and it releases it is heavy enough to go flying across the platters and destroy the surface on them and any data with it.

I recommend gently prying up on the rear of the magnet with a small flat head screwdriver while securely holding the magnet with your hand or a pair of needle nose pliers.

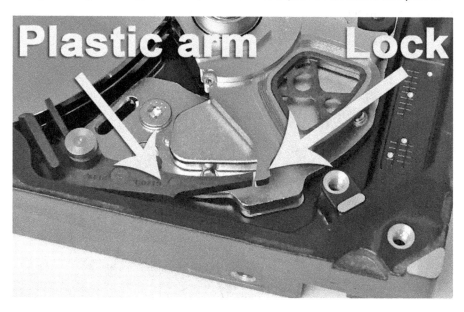

Now there is a plastic lock on the left of the arm you can gently push away from the arm. This allows you to turn the arm assembly all the way so that the heads come off the platters. You want to do this very slowly and carefully so that you do not scratch anything or let the heads crash into anything including each other.

With the heads away from the platter you can use a flat head screwdriver to loosen the center retaining bolt from the arm assembly. Now remove the screws on the left and right side of the arm assembly's base, rotating the heads as necessary to gain access to the screws.

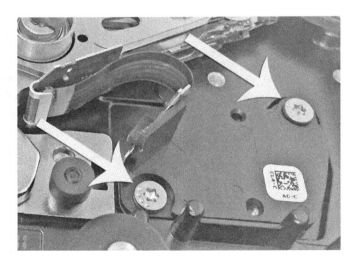

The arm assembly is attached to something with a cable and in this case that plate is held down with two screws which we can remove now. This plate is a pain to remove as it needs to slide straight off.

You can make this easier on some drives by removing the board from the back of the drive and gently pushing on the connector that goes inside the drive (arrow in the right image above).

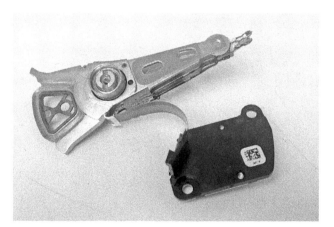 

The arm assembly should now be free to remove from the drive. Note in the picture above right that the head on the far left is missing which explains why this drive failed.

To install a new arm assembly simply reverse this procedure paying particular attention to the heads when you rotate the arm assembly, getting the heads back on the platters. Never move the heads on the platters any more than is absolutely required to do the job and never any further away from the edge than is required to get them to sit flush on the platters.

Close the drive back up as quickly as possible and make sure all the screws are very snug and use a pattern to snug them. By pattern I mean never snug down two next to each other, do one corner, then the opposite corner, and then move to the right of the first one, and then to the right of the second one, etc. This makes sure the cover is perfectly flat as you close it. I choose the word snug intentionally as I did not mean tight. If you strip one of these it can warp the cover or leave a gap making the drive fail faster. If it works at all you will only get a short time to recover your data so we need to have as much time as possible.

That's it. Plug it in and try it. If you are really lucky it might actually work.

4.6 Optical media recovery

Optical media has very few options for recovery. Fortunately if handled reasonably well it is not often necessary to perform recovery on optical media as it is a very robust and reliable format that can withstand an amazing amount of punishment and still last years. For the purposes of this section we will be working with a data CDROM however the ideas presented here will work equally well for DVD media in virtually any format.

Before you do anything else you should clean the disc using a towel dampened with warm water and inspect it. Never use any form of cleaners or abrasives up front, just clean off the fingerprints and any grime that may be there. Some people never think to clean a disc and even if that does not solve your problem it keeps you from sticking a disc with an unknown sticky substance inside your optical drive. Ick!

Should the disc have any cracks in it be warned that when a disc spins up to full speed it is completely possible that the disc will shatter. If this happens not only might you wind up with a drive full of small sharp plastic pieces but it could also destroy the drive. If you must try a disc that has a crack you can use a cheap drive that you do not mind being trashed and you can also sometimes restrict the maximum speed the drive will read at which lessens the odds of a catastrophic failure.

The second thing I always do is to try the media in another optical reader. You would be amazed at how often a different reader will read media that the first reader will not. I often try reading CDs in DVD drives and even BD drives with great success. It seems that DVDRW drives tend to read the greatest variety of discs so I always try those for everything except BDs which a DVD drive will of course not read.

Back in the days of floppy disks it was common for the cheaper disk drives to warp over time and refuse to read disks that it had created previously. Putting the disk in a different drive often solved this issue and would read the disk perfectly. Although optical drives do not tend to warp like this, it is still possible for the laser to be weaker or less aligned in one drive as compared to another so it never hurts to try.

Failing that the next most likely thing is that the bottom (the side that does not have the label on it) is severely scratched. As long as we are talking scratches and not huge gouges then there is still a good chance that you can recover data from the disc.

Remember back in the section on media when discussing optical media types I mentioned that the data is actually located closer to the label side of the disc than the bottom, even though it is read through the bottom. This means that as long as the label side is in reasonable shape and the bottom is not severely damaged then you might can clean up the bottom and read the data.

In order to "clean up" the bottom you actually need to polish it. There are many varieties of polishers out there by many different names but you need to make sure you get something that either specifically mentions polishing or repairing and not just a cleaner. This can be confusing because I have seen cleaners and polishers that look almost identical and even have very similar wording on the box. Sometimes you will see cleaners marketed as being able to restore your ability to read a disc but reading the fine print will tell you that it just gives it a good cleaning.

This is the polisher I use, the SkipDr DVD and CD Manual Disc Repair System which is available on Amazon for less than $20. It does a pretty good job. You simply spray the liquid it comes with on the disc, insert it into the cleaner and spin the knob on the other side. It rotates and polishes the disc at the same time so all you have to do is crank. They say to not use this on Blu-Ray discs however some people say it works. They do make a version for Blu-Rays so I would probably get the correct one if I was working on a Blu-Ray.

Before I polished the disc it looked like this:

After a few spins in the polisher it looked like this:

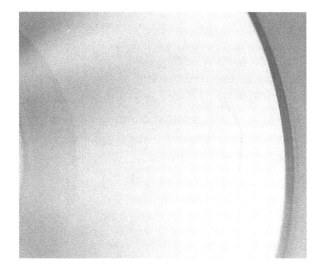

Perfect? No, notice the large scratch is still there on the right close to the outside edge. But also note that most of the scratches are completely gone and even that large scratch is substantially diminished. More importantly I have been able to polish discs and read them to get a customer's data off where they could not. Happy customer means it was worth it.

Part 5: Deleted partition recovery

On Windows PCs I have run into many situations where the hard drive has somehow had its partitions removed. Of course the drive will not boot, there is no data and the customer never has any idea what happened.

When you insert the drive and look at it in Windows Disk Management tool you see the following image:

It is just all gone. Fortunately this is a pretty easy thing to fix with the right tools, and I like Active@ Partition Recovery (www.partition-recovery.com). They have a free version that will show you what it can see but to recover the data you need at least the standard version which will set you back about $40. The professional version has some nice features and only costs $10 more so I prefer that. If you do one recovery with this software it easily pays for itself.

First thing, never try this while the drive is still in the customer's machine. If it was a hardware problem such as a controller error, attempting a recovery may just make things worse. Pull the drive and work on it in another computer. Make sure that your antivirus is up to date in the computer you decide to use just in case it was a virus or piece of spyware that caused the problem (very rare but entirely possible and it is better to be safe than to have the same thing happen to your computer too).

Once you install the software and launch it, the drive you are working on will show up on the left side while data about it shows on the right as shown below.

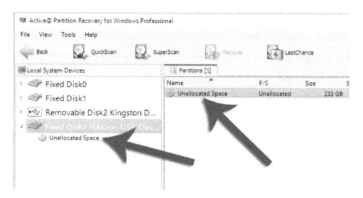

Note that it shows just like Windows that all partitions and data are gone. Start by clicking the picture of the hard drive that says QuickScan near the top left and let it do its scan. Once the initial scan is complete it will show you a listing of partitions it found and their condition over in the left hand pane.

Note in this screen shot above that there are three partitions in excellent condition and one in very bad condition. The good news is that the DellUtility partition is not required for getting this user's data or even restoring the data to a bootable state. If I restore the first three partitions the drive should be perfectly usable. You can now click on a partition and it will do a more in-depth scan of that partition.

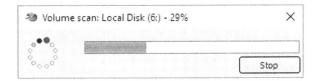

It then displays all the files and directories it found over on the right hand pane. Use this to make sure the files you need are there before performing the recovery by clicking on the recover button near the top center of the screen.

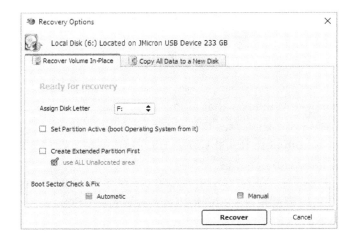

The recovery screen will pop up when you click the recover button and it is shown here. Normally this is all you need and you can recover the entire drive right there. Remember to select the checkbox for the bootable partition to make it active.

There may be cases where you are not sure what may be where or the partitions you need may not be the ones in excellent condition, in those cases you can click the tab on the top labeled Copy All Data to a New Disk to see this next screen.

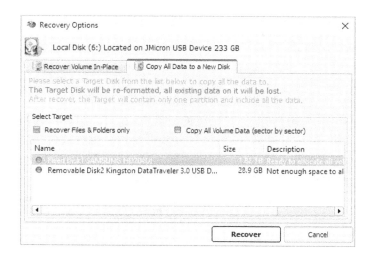

Here you can select where you want the partition to be restored. Once you select any and all options you want, simply click the Recover button and watch it do its magic.

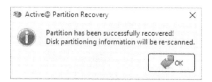

Once the program has finished it will pop up a box telling you it has completed.

In this case I only needed the data off the drive so I only restored the largest partition. Here you can see that Windows now sees it in the Windows Disk Management utility and more importantly...

It shows up as a drive that I can access in Windows file explorer.

Once you have the drive back to the way it should be you should start running tests to see what made the partitions disappear in the first place. I highly recommend you start with antivirus and antimalware scans and then move on to hardware tests on the drive and controller.

A common reason for this to happen, at least with my past customers, is they decide they want to reinstall their operating system or to install a new operating system over the old. Many of the recovery media and new installation discs tend to just delete all the partitions and create new ones rather than use any of the old ones. This tends to overwrite the drive in such a way as you cannot restore it to a usable and bootable state, but you can often get the data off the drive such as their pictures, music and documents.

In the shop a common problem is that I recycle disks using one as a clone disk over and over. Every once in a while I overwrite a drive. I use a hard drive as a clone drive for one customer and then overwrite it with another clone from a different customer, and then need something back for the first customer. While it doesn't always work it has helped me restore data in that situation more than once.

We previously talked about Partition Guru in the deleted file recovery section and you may notice that it too has the ability to search for and restore deleted partitions. You may be asking why since I use it for one thing but use a different program here. The answer is simple, it doesn't work as well at this particular job.

To give you an example, when I look at the same drive that we just looked at it shows only two partitions instead of the four that Active@ found. It is also not quite as fast and easy in my experience.

To be totally honest, both programs found the partition I needed and restored them in almost the same time with the same end results. If however I was wanting to restore this drive to a completely bootable state, Partition Guru would have failed because it did not find one of the system reserved partitions that Windows needed to boot whereas Active@ found it immediately with the quick scan.

Part 6: Virus/Spyware/Crypto data recovery

The first thing I want to do is define what I mean by each type of infection.

A virus is a piece of software with two distinct traits; to cause damage to a system and to replicate. That damage could be anything from deleting files, removing partitions, or stopping the machine from getting on the internet. The author wants to cause damage, havoc or general mischief. You will probably never see a virus except on a Windows computer and then only rarely these days.

Spyware (or malware, MALicious softWARE) is software written with the intent for the author to make money. This can be accomplished by stealing your banking information, stealing account passwords, displaying advertisements, redirecting you to websites they profit from, collecting information about your shopping or surfing habits for resale, tricking you into thinking you have system problems and getting you to call "tech support", and much more. Spyware is rampant on Windows machines, and not uncommon on Macs and Android devices.

Crypo (more commonly called ransomware) is software that encrypts your data and will not let you have it back unless you pay them money. They typically give you a few days to pay them and they want payment in an anonymous payment method such as Bitcoin or Moneypack. If you fail to pay within the given time frame they delete the decryption key and your data is permanently lost. Crypto is primarily on Windows machines however there have been verified cases of it appearing on Macs as well.

While we are discussing this, one term you may run into while cleaning up your computers might be PUPs (Potentially Unwanted Programs). These are programs that are not necessarily spyware, certainly not viruses, but may have been installed without your consent (well, technically you did consent you just didn't know you did).

When you download some pieces of software, primarily free software, they may "bundle" other software with it. For example downloading Adobe Air or updates for Air bundles Google Chrome and wants to change your default web browser (and may change your home page as well). If you are one of those people who just clicks next, next, next while installing software instead of carefully reading each screen you could get a lot of PUPs installed alongside your legitimate software you intended.

Sometimes like in the case of Adobe software as long as you read each screen it is pretty easy to avoid this. With some software from other companies there is no easy way to avoid the installation of PUPs unless you choose something like the custom or advanced installation when you start the installation process and then step through all the configuration options.

While PUPs may not be spyware or viruses they can still contribute substantially to a cluttered and slow computer. You can manually uninstall these by going through the add/remove programs feature of Windows, or for Mac simply drag the app to the trash and empty it.

If for whatever reason on a Mac the normal method does not work or leaves behind files use something like AppCleaner (www.freemacsoft.net/appcleaner/) to help you clean it up.

Spyware is by far the biggest problem we face today by volume while crypto is the most dangerous. Viruses have pretty much disappeared for the most part.

Recovering data from a typical virus or spyware infection is usually pretty straight forward. You clean off the infection and your data is still there completely intact. While that sounds easy enough it can be a little more difficult to do than it is to say. Let's take a look at some basic ways you can remove this nasty software from your computer.

The first program I tell people to run is MalwareBytes AntiMalware (www.malwarebytes.org). For home users it is a free download and is an excellent program to run first. Not only does it do a fine job at removing the vast majority of spyware I run into on a daily basis but it is an excellent gauge of how infected the machine is. If you find virtually nothing with this, odds are the machine is pretty clean. If you find thousands of problems with it, then there is an excellent chance there are more serious problems.

The second program I recommend people run is Kaspersky's TDSS Killer (www.bleepingcomputer.com/download/tdsskiller/). It rarely finds anything but it takes seconds to run, is totally free, and finds things many other programs will not.

If there are still more problems, next I recommend MalwareBytes AntiRootkit (www.malwarebytes.org). This is a program that as its name suggests is aimed at rootkits. Rootkits are difficult for some programs to find and remove so this specialized tool comes in very handy.

Next up is HitmanPro (www.surfright.nl/en/hitmanpro). The free version will allow you to scan and find any problems. To remove the problems you will need to purchase a license. If you are still having problems and this finds infections it is well worth the price.

The last thing I recommend as a matter of course is an actual antivirus, assuming the machine does not have one installed, running and up to date, or if the one installed is not a good product. There are many antiviruses you could use including trial versions of Kaspersky (www.kaspersky.com) or Norton (www.norton.com). If you are looking for a free version you could try Avira (www.avira.com) or Panda (www.pandasecurity.com) free versions.

If you still have problems it is time to use the web and talk to professionals to help narrow down your problem. Anything past this point may require things such as booting into safe mode, registry editing and manually deleting files. Best case scenario may be that they simply tell you to run another program to remove the infection as there are hundreds of programs out there. A great place to find help is www.bleepingcomputer.com.

Once the infection is gone you should be able to safely use your files again or if necessary you can undelete any files that the infection may have deleted.

Crypto is a different beast. You have two choices when dealing with this type of infection: pay them or restore the files from backup. Decrypting the files yourself could potentially take hundreds of years of computer time, if not more, so that is not a realistic option.

Should you pay them? I hate the idea. Paying them only perpetuates the cycle and makes sure they will continue doing this to people. The other side is that everyone that pays on time, gets their data back. Let me clarify that last statement....

To my knowledge, every person or organization that has paid the requested amount in the requested time period has been able to decrypt their data and get it all back. I have heard many stories of so-and-so's brother's friend's next door neighbor's dog's aunt's wife not getting their data back, but no credible direct evidence. In fact, several police departments and a hospital have been in the news as paying the ransom and getting their data back.

One word of warning however: if your antivirus software removes the infection you may not be able to get the data back even if you do pay. The first thing you should do once you know you have been infected and your files are encrypted is to turn off your antivirus or other security software. I know this sounds counter-intuitive but that software is normally required to decrypt the data and if it is deleted you may be out of luck.

Let's assume that you have decided not to pay, or waited too long or your security software deleted the required decryption software and you need to try to recover what you can.

The first thing to do is restore from your backups (keeping in mind that you should never restore from backups or even look at your backups until you are sure the infection is removed). If you do not have backups we need to be a little more resourceful.

Sending your drive in for data recovery at this point will not help, the files were not deleted they were encrypted. Taking your computer to a computer repair shop will not help either, they can't decrypt the data either however they should be able to make sure the infection is gone.

The last ditch effort is to use Window's shadow copy service to restore some data. Assuming you are running a modern version of Windows and are installed on a drive formatted in NTFS, you can use software such as Z-VSScopy (from www.z-dbackup.com) to restore shadow copies of files on your drive. I have actually had this work quite well although more often than not it does not work at all. If you were infected with Locky this trick will not work because Locky specifically targets and removes the VSS files.

On a Mac you can restore from your Time Machine or if running the new Sierra there should be snapshots and previous versions of files you can restore. Unfortunately it is such a new operating system that there are currently no tools out yet to help much with it.

Part 7: Preventing future data loss

No matter how good your techniques, or how good your recovery software, you will never be as good as if you prevented the data loss in the first place. Of course if you are reading this book it may be a little late for that.

If you are planning on doing this professionally then you can make a tidy sum by selling backup solutions, NASs (Network Attached Storage) and RAID (Redundant Array of Inexpensive Disks) setups, all of which we will talk about in this section. In addition, you could even become a reseller for cloud backup solutions such as Mosey.

Selling these products and services to your clients will not only get you income, it will make your customers very pleased when the unspeakable happens and your solutions save the day.

If you are not doing this professionally, think of the satisfaction you will derive from having excellent backups and getting everything back quickly when your hard drive fails or some other catastrophe befalls you.

7.1 Backup strategies

I am constantly amazed at how many people have no backups of their data. Some people seem to think data loss won't ever happen to them, through ignorance or arrogance I couldn't tell you. Other people honestly do not think their data is that important until they lose it. The really scary part is backups can be very easy and inexpensive to do. Let's take a look.

Let's start by defining what exactly a backup is, and is not. In order to be a backup, the data must exist in two places. Moving your pictures off of your computer onto an external hard drive sold as a backup drive is not a backup. Moving your data off your computer onto a cloud backup service is not a backup. Think of it like a duplicate of a piece of paper. It cannot be a duplicate if there are not two of them.

So why do we need backups? For starters hard drives fail, often. I am writing this at lunch after just replacing a hard drive in a customer's server. Fortunately the server had a RAID which means they did not lose any data. We have a huge stack of hard drives in the office that have failed and that stack is just the ones for the past few months, previous ones were recycled. When a drive fails you may or may not be able to recover any data. We are usually pretty fortunate in that we can recover quite a bit of data but it is certainly not uncommon for the drive to lose everything.

The next main reason to keep backups is encryption malware like Cryptolocker commonly called ransomware. This software manages to encrypt all your user files (documents, spreadsheets, presentations, pictures, music, video, data files like Quickbooks and much more) and force you to pay a ransom to get it unencrypted. One such case in the news recently was a hospital in California which was forced to pay $17,000 to recover all their data including medical charts, patient data, billing information, test results, etc. How much backup could you buy for $17,000? My office deals with a few of these infections every month.

How about protection from accidental deletion? Have you ever deleted a file you didn't mean to? I know I certainly have. Having good backups means if this happens you can easily restore the deleted file and move on.

Now that we know what a backup is and why we need them, let us look at the easiest way to backup our data. Cloud backup services such as Carbonite (www.carbonite.com), Sugarsync (www.sugarsync.com) and CrashPlan (www.crashplan.com) allow you to have all the data on your computer backed up to the cloud automatically. As soon as you create a new document, it is uploaded to the cloud. They also normally provide versioning which means if one of your files gets corrupted, infected or encrypted you can restore a previous version before the problem happened.

The only logical reason I know of not to run an online backup service is if you have hundreds of gigabytes of data that needs to be backed up. It could be extremely slow to move this much data over the internet unless you have an extremely fast internet connection. Remember that by fast connection I am talking about the speed at which you can upload data, not download it. Most internet plans have a substantially faster download speed than upload speed. For example my home internet now is 50Mb down but only 5-10Mb up and I consider my upload speed very fast considering other plans in my area.

For one of my customers I installed an online cloud backup program and started the upload. Their 1.5Mb download .25Mb upload connection was 15% of the way done with the initial backup a week later when I checked back. At this rate they might get it all uploaded in a little over a month.

Now let's discuss the different types of local backups; images, full, differential and incremental.

Image backups are just like the clones we discussed earlier except the clone is to a file. Think of it as scanning a piece of paper into a computer as a PDF. That PDF can be used to create an exact duplicate of the original piece of paper if you print it, or you can just read the PDF to get the information out you need.

An image is the same. You can restore the image to the original hard drive or a different hard drive to make an exact duplicate of the original. This means your operating system, programs, and data are exactly as they were when you made the image. Some programs even allow you to restore this image to a computer with different hardware which usually causes problems because the image does not have the drivers for the new hardware installed.

Images can also be backed up just like file backups as full images, differential or incremental.

Full backups are backups of everything you tell it to back up. Every time you run the backup, everything is backed up. You can run a full backup of only selected files such as your pictures and that means that all your pictures will be backed up every time you run the backup.

Differential backups are when the program backs up everything that is different since the last time a full backup has been run. It only looks at the last full backup, not the last differential. If your last full backup was ten days ago and you do a differential every day, and a file was changed one time eight days ago then you will have that file backed up in the full backup and eight out of the nine differential backups.

Incremental backups are when the program backs up everything that is different since the last backup was run, either a full or incremental. Using the same scenario as we discussed in differential backups the file that was changed would be backed up in the original full backup and then in the second incremental, and only in that incremental until it is changed again.

Full backups offer the best protection from things like ransomware and failed or corrupt backups but use the most time and storage space.

The online route is indeed the easiest, and the local route is the most flexible, but what is the best? Let's assume you run a business or have data that is critical that it not be lost. What is the best method for protecting that?

The general rule is the 3-2-1 rule. This rule states that you have three backups, on two different types of media, one of which is offsite. Let's break this down.

Why three backups? Because it is entirely possible that two of your backups have a problem such as failed drives or they burned up with the computers in your office when it caught fire. Making sure there are three gives you double redundancy and this means it would be virtually impossible for you to lose your data.

Now we come to two different types of media. This means that you should not keep all your backups on external hard drives, or all on DVDs. This protects you against the possibility that your backup media is no longer readable through technology advances, and also as some media such as DVDs have a finite lifespan. Think of all the people who archived their documents to ZIP disks, or Jazz drives, or DLT tapes. How would you restore those backups? Don't even know what those are? Kinda makes my point doesn't it?

Lastly is the keeping of one backup offsite. In the case of a fire, flood or burglary you might lose everything at that location. Keeping one copy off site makes sure that does not happen. Using a cloud backup service is perfect for offsite backup, as would be a backup hard drive of your office data kept at your house. I do recommend that if you are keeping an offsite copy that the copy not be next door, in the same apartment complex or in any way in close proximity to another backup copy. An exception to this might be if you keep a copy in a safe deposit box of a bank that is next door.

Using the 321 backup strategy virtually guarantees that you will always have that data but there is another problem that virtually no one ever thinks about. Are the backups any good? Have you actually restored data from them? If not, then you do not know if the backup is any good.

Backups are only as good as the last time you checked them, tested them, and verified them. Make this a scheduled event in your calendar. I have a list at home of things I do once a month. This includes things like charge my emergency battery pack, swap rechargeable batteries on my handheld amateur radios, doing virus/malware scans on my computers, and checking my backups. This also makes sure that if a disaster strikes, you are ready to recover your data instead of fumbling with instruction manuals and technical support phone calls to India.

So what are some good ideas for backups? Do you need the best for a few pictures of your cat? Actually, that depends on your cat, heh.

Determining how much backup you need can be tough. I normally assess what would happen if the data was lost and then decide how much time, effort and money I think that customer would be willing to invest to stop the worst from happening.

For the typical home user who has a few pictures, documents and maybe a video of the family vacation who would not be too devastated if it all went away, I sometimes recommend an online backup solution and a large USB thumb drive. The thumb drive they can keep in a drawer in case the hard drive fails and then the cloud backup is in case the house burns down. While not as good as the 321 system it should be more than sufficient for most families.

If they have a more extensive photo collection and some serious documents that would be difficult or impossible to reproduce, then I add an external hard drive backup to the mix. Both Windows and Mac computers have backup software built in. This provides all the requirements for the 321 system with offsite cloud backup, USB thumb drive, and external hard drive.

If you need a few more configuration options and capabilities than the built in backup solutions in Windows you could try software such as Z-DBackup (www.z-dbackup.com). Z-DBackup is an excellent product allowing for very simple, or very complex configurations. It is also free for private home users and very inexpensive for commercial use for what it can do.

For even more protection such as for a business we may suggest two external hard drives and a more robust backup software package such as the previously mentioned Z-DBackup or EaseUS Todo Backup (www.easus.com). EaseUS makes versions for home users and business users with prices to match. The advantage here is that they can keep a complete snapshot of the drive which can be restored at one time, or you can restore a single file, with anything in between. The more expensive versions even allow you to restore a complete system image to a completely different computer which is very helpful if the entire machine fails or burns.

Often these business customers may have more data than could be reasonably uploaded to a cloud backup solution. One such customer has literally millions of files occupying terabytes of storage. For them I recommended two large capacity external hard drives that are rotated every week along with EaseUS Todo Backup for servers. One of those two hard drives are kept off site in a fireproof safe and are swapped out every week.

Unfortunately this customer does not have three different backups or two different media types but that is a concession we had to make due to the mass volume of data. Simply making a single image of his data takes around six hours across a USB3 connection and is a single 1.5TB file. To offset this, the backups are checked very often.

For Macs we have already talked about cloning software and both the products I mentioned (Carbon Copy Cloner and SuperDuper) have excellent backup facilities built right in. The Time Machine solution provided by Apple is an excellent solution but for even more flexibility you can use either of these cloning software packages for excellent results.

Always be thinking of what would happen if you lost everything and when that happens, what you would be willing to do to get it back. Find a good balance between time, effort and expense now to prevent disaster later.

7.1.1 Z-DBackup (Windows)

Z-DBackup is a fairly full featured backup program for Windows. To make it even better it is free for private, non-commercial use. It can make complete disk images or just backup your data and it can do both very efficiently. Storage for your backups can be locally to external drives, secondary internal drives, network locations and even to FTP sites, it really is flexible.

Once you download and install the software you will see the following screen when you run it.

This screen shows the current backup sets that have been created. Since we just installed the software, nothing is shown. Click the Backup icon near the top left where you will be presented with the following screen.

Virtually everyone will want to select the top option here for Data Backup – Wizard to start with. Later on if you want more advanced functions you can select Windows System Image to make a complete image of the drive or the last option for more control over your backups.

Here you can put whatever name you like in the Name section, being incredibly creative as I am I used the name "Backup". Next use the dropdown box titled Select to select where you will be putting the backup. I backed up to an external USB hard drive. Click Next.

Here you are presented with a list of all the directories on your hard drive where you can select what you want to back up. I recommend you backup only items in your profile and only the directories such as Documents, Music, Photos, etc. Attempting to back up the entire users directory might cause problems and will certainly backup more than you really want, however it will guarantee that you get all your data if you stored everything in the normal places.

Z-DBackup now presents you with a screen showing all the places you want to back up. If this is correct, click Next.

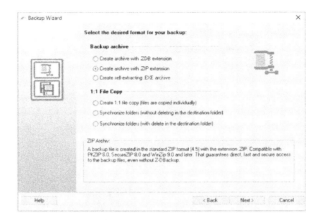

Here you find options on how you want to store your backup and whether you want to make a backup archive file or do a simple file copy. I tend to prefer ZIP archives for my normal backups but I also use the Synchronize folders options sometimes to make backups of hard drives such as my photographs. Make your selection and click Next.

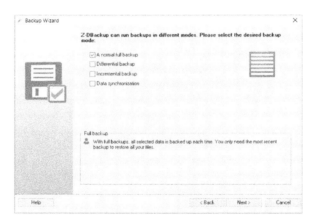

If you selected for the software to make a backup archive file, then you will be presented with the options shown above. I prefer the first option most of the time because this allows me to have multiple backups of each file. Differential and Incremental options both only backup things that have changed, and if one backup archive becomes corrupt or deleted I may not have another copy of a specific file.

Make your selection and click Next.

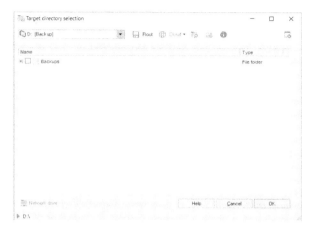

This screen allows you to select where exactly you want to store your backups. Use the dropdown box at the top to select the drive and then browse in the bottom box to find the directory where you want to put the backup files. Now click the box to the left of the directory you want and click OK.

Since the external hard drive I am using is formatted in FAT32 which does not support files larger than 2GB it asks me if I want to create large files. I do not so I select No. This should split the backup files into files just under 2GB so I can move them around on any file system I want.

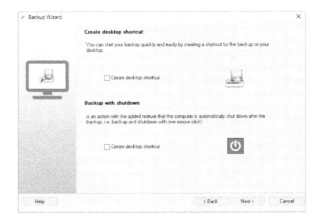

This screen allows you to create desktop shortcuts that you can later just double click on to run a backup. This is an excellent option when you are synchronizing files on your computer to an external hard drive or NAS. For scheduled backups however, this really doesn't do much although it does make a nice way to force a backup. Once done, click Next.

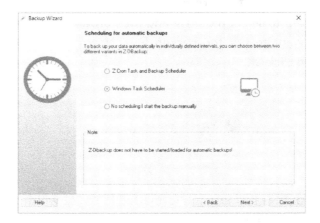

Now we come to the screen where we can choose to start the scheduling options or to not schedule the backup. I normally like to choose the Windows Task Scheduler option in the center as it keeps all my scheduled tasks in one place. Once ready, click on Next.

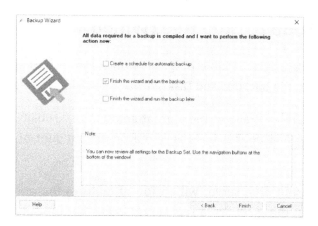

I always select the center option to Finish the wizard and run the backup. This option makes sure the backup works as intended instead of finding out about it much later, or not at all. Running the backup now makes sure that the options I selected are correct, the media I want to use is connected correctly and that the media is good. Select your choice and click Next.

The program now verifies that I want to run the backup now so I select Yes.

The next screen shown is the program actually running the backup and its progress. Once complete the software will let you know what happened so you are not surprised. Overall a pretty straight forward wizard and a good software package.

7.1.2 EaseUS Todo Backup free (Windows)

EaseUS Todo Backup is a very capable program with a ton of backup options. We will be discussing two options, file backups and Disk/Partition backups, both scheduled.

I really like this software as it allows me a great amount of flexibility in what I want to do (clone, backup, image) and does it for a very reasonable amount of money (starting with free).

Even if you need to use it on a server with a ton of features the price is still a reasonable $200 as of today. Trust me, $200 for a real server image backup solution that will back up to external drives and even across the network is an awesome value.

7.1.2.1 File Backups with Todo Backup

File backups are the most common type of backup and they backup your data files such as documents, music, photos, and videos. Let's start by opening the program...

and clicking on File Backup near the top left.

Here we see a host of options and most of them are already filled in for us. Click the Library folder in the upper left and make sure that Music, Pictures and Videos are selected if you want those backed up. You can also browse to any folder on your hard drive and select it.

Now look at the area where it says Destination and use the folder icon on the far right of that line to see the file explorer.

Use this window to select where you want to store your backups and then click OK at the bottom. Once back at the previous screen you can enter a Plan name and Description if you want, or you can leave them as default.

Now click on the Scheduling: Off at the bottom left.

Here you can select when you want the backups to run, what kind of backups they are and other options. I recommend running the backups daily at a specific time like 2am and making them incremental while waking up the computer and running missed backups.

I should note that incremental backups are the most efficient in hard drive space used and speed but do not protect as well from ransomware. If you are concerned with ransomware and this is your only backup method, then you should select "Full backup" from the drop down box instead of "Incremental backup". When finished select Save.

The next screen you see shows the backup set you just created and allows you to recover, backup or change the options etc. I highly recommend you attempt to run a backup now by clicking the backup button and selecting Full from the menu that drops down.

Once it starts the backup it will show you the progress along with the estimated time remaining as well as giving you the ability to change a few options or cancel the current backup.

7.1.2.2 Disk/Partition backups with Todo Backup

One of my favorite backup methods is a full image backup. The reason I like them is because I have a complete backup of everything made, in my case, three times a week so if any file has a problem I have several copies I can restore from.

This means that if I do a backup on Monday and then get infected with ransomware on Tuesday which I do not detect, then all my files are encrypted and backed up Wednesday I can still restore from either Monday's backup or Friday's backup.

I can also do a complete system restore and make sure absolutely everything is restored in one pass instead of having to figure out what is and is not messed up and restoring that as I go. Much easier.

The down side, and there is always a down side, is that it takes a lot more hard drive space to store the backups and a lot more time to create them. I have large external hard drives and my backups run over USB3 in the middle of the night while I am sleeping so neither of those two things are really big issues for me.

You start at the same screen as before.

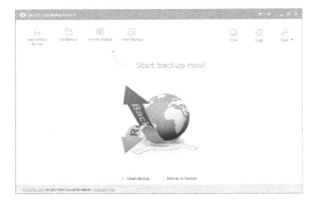

Here we will click on the top left icon that says Disk/Partition Backup.

On this screen instead of selecting the files we want in the top section we select the hard drive, or partitions, we want to back up. In this case I have selected the entire hard drive by checking the box at the very top. If you have multiple hard drives you can just scroll down to find the one you want to back up.

Now look at the area where it says Destination and use the folder icon on the far right of that line to see the file explorer.

Use this window to select where you want to store your backups and then click OK at the bottom. Once back at the previous screen you can enter a Plan name and Description if you want, or you can leave them as default.

Now click on the Scheduling: Off at the bottom left.

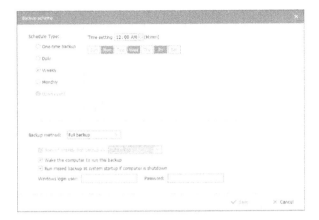

Here you can select when you want the backups to run, what kind of backups they are and other options. I recommend running the backups as often as your hard drive space allows at a specific time like 2am and making them full backups.

If you have limited space to store the backups you can use incremental but that does not give you the same benefits as doing multiple full backups.

Next click on Save and then when back on the main Disk/Partition Backup screen, click on Image-reserve strategy near the bottom center.

Here are the options for keeping a certain number of backups. I typically set this to three but you can keep more or less depending on how much free space you have where you will be storing the backups. Normally you will want enough space for one more full backup than you really want because it will create the new backup and then delete the oldest one. You want this behavior so that it makes sure there is a good new one before deleting a good old one.

Click on Save when you are done and then Save on the main Disk/Partition Backup screen.

The next screen you see shows the backup set you just created and allows you to recover, backup or change the options etc. I highly recommend you attempt to run a backup now by clicking the backup button and selecting Full from the menu that drops down.

Once it starts the backup it will show you the progress along with the estimated time remaining as well as giving you the ability to change a few options or cancel the current backup.

7.1.3 Time Machine (Mac)

If you are doing regular scheduled backups of your Mac it is hard to beat the built in Time Machine program provided by Apple. To start with, there is nothing to download and setup could not be much easier. I grabbed an old Western Digital 500GB USB2 drive to show you the setup from start to finish.

First I plugged in the hard drive but since it was set up for a Windows machine I needed to format it so I opened Disk Utility on the Mac. I selected the new drive on the left pane and right clicked on it.

On this menu I clicked on the bottom option to Erase.

I gave it a name, in this case Mac Backup, then selected Mac OS Extended (Journaled) from the Format drop down list and clicked Erase.

Once the format was complete the system automatically popped this box up asking me if I wanted to use this new drive as a Time Machine backup, how did they know? I clicked the bottom right button labeled Use as Backup Disk.

The next screen that appeared allowed me to modify any options (I didn't as there really isn't anything to modify) and started a countdown. Once that countdown from about 90 seconds ran all the way to zero it started the backup automatically.

Time Machine automatically keeps hourly backups of changes for the past 24 hours, daily backups for the past month and weekly backups for all previous months as long as it has hard drive space. Once the space is exhausted and the drive becomes full the oldest backups are deleted to make room for the new backups.

That is just about the perfect backup scenario.

Once your initial backup finishes you should see the following screen:

This screen shows you the amount of space used on your backup drive, the oldest backup, the latest backup and the next time that a backup will run. You can close this window and the backups will happen automatically without another thought from you.

7.1.4 fwbackups (Linux)

There are a lot of options when it comes to backups for Linux, my personal choice is fwbackups (www.diffingo.com). It is an easy, fast and reliable solution for file backups which is pretty much all I do on Linux.

 If your Linux distribution has fwbackups available you can install it that way and make your life a little easier. I run Ubuntu and it does not have it so I had to go to diffingo.com and download the source tarball. The instructions that follow are for Ubuntu 16.04 LTS so there may be variations for your specific distro and version.

Once you have it downloaded open a terminal window and change to your Downloads directory and run the following commands:

```
sudo apt-get install gettext autotools-dev intltool python-crypto python-paramiko python-gtk2 python-glade2 python-notify cron

tar xfj fwbackups-1.43.6.tar.bz2

cd fwbackups-1.43.6

./configure --prefix=/usr

make && sudo make install
```

Of course the archive name of fwbackups-1.43.6 should reflect the version you have downloaded. 1.43.6 just happens to be the most current as of this writing.

Once the software is installed you can run it and get the following screen.

From this screen you can select either Backup Sets which is where you set up scheduled file backups or One-Time Backup if you only want to run one backup and be done. Let's select Backup Sets and schedule a backup.

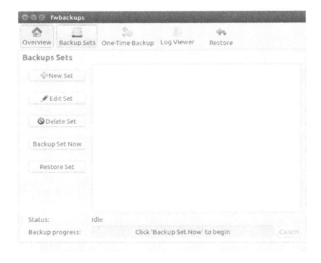

From this screen we click on New Set near the top left side.

On this screen we enter a name for the backup (I used the name "Backup" just to be original) and select to add either files or folders by using the buttons on the left. Note that I have already selected my home directory which is all I will be backing up.

You can move along the tabs at the top of the screen and select the Destination next.

On this tab you can use the browse button over on the right to select where you will store your backup. In this case I am putting it on an external USB drive named BACKUP. Now click on the Times tab.

This tab allows us to set the schedule of how often we want to run the backups. Once you set your options here you can click on the Options (Simple) tab.

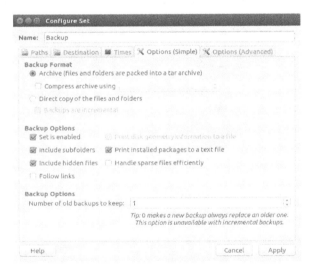

I almost always leave all the options alone unless I have a specific need to change them. The one exception is the last option, Number of old backups to keep, which I normally set to three just because I like that number. Next you can click on the last Options tab.

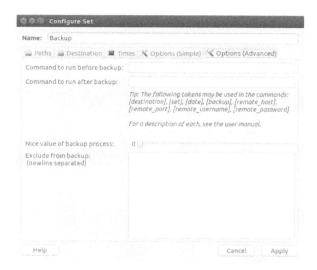

I can honestly say I have never used this tab but you may find it useful if you need to fire off another process as soon as the backup completes. Once you are done here click the Apply button at the bottom right and it will take you back to the first screen with one difference...

You now have a backup set. Click on the icon for the Backup backup set (or whatever you called yours) and then you can click over on the left, Backup Set Now to start the backup.

The above screen appears and the backup process starts. Once it is complete you hopefully see the screen below.

That's it, you're done. You should now have scheduled file backups going all the time and always have a current backup. Be sure to check your backups periodically so you know they are good, preferably before a disaster strikes and you need them.

7.2 RAIDs

A RAID is a Redundant Array of Inexpensive Disks, or in something a little easier to understand, a bunch of hard drives arranged in such a way that if one fails you do not lose any data (or, in such a manner to increase speed). This allows you to replace the failed drive and continue on as if nothing happened. Sounds pretty simple, it isn't.

There are several types of RAIDs, each providing different capabilities and functions. Let's take a look and see how a few of them work.

RAID 0: This type of RAID is for speed, not data redundancy. By taking two hard drives and "striping" them (writing half the data to one and the other half to the second) you allow the writing of data twice as fast, in theory. In reality you do get a huge boost in both read and write speed but the overhead in processing the data eats up some of the time you theoretically would have gained. You still get a nice boost in performance but you are now **twice as likely to lose data** because if either of the two drives fail you lose everything.

RAID 1: This RAID configuration takes two drives and mirrors them. Whatever is written to one is also written to the other at the same instant. This slows things down just a little as there is some processing involved in duplicating the data but if either drive fails you can continue working uninterrupted as if nothing happened, in theory. In reality if one drive fails the whole process gets slower as the RAID controller and operating system try to figure out what the heck is going on with the failed drive. Still, you do not lose any data.

RAID 5: Three or more drives can be combined to make a RAID 5. This has two advantages; first that the more drives you install the faster it can read and write data, and the second is it being possible to configure a RAID 5 so that you could in theory have two hard drives fail and not lose data. This is done with what is called a "hot spare" which will instantly take over once a failed drive is detected. The theory is that if one drive fails the hot spare will take over, making it as if no drive has failed. Then, if a second drive fails you in theory only have one drive that is not working.

Think of this, you have a three drive RAID 5 (drives 1-3) with a hot spare (drive 4). Drive one fails which causes drive 4 to kick into action. Now you have a three drive RAID 5 consisting of drives 2-4 with drive 1 being dead. Then drive 3 fails and you have only two working drives which is enough to keep your data intact.

The way this works is that each drive is divided into data and parity stripe sections. In the event of a drive failure the parity stripe from the remaining drives can be combined to recreate the data from the missing drive.

Speed is increased because when a 1MB file is sent to the array, for three drives it is split into three sections and written to all three drives at the same time. The more drives, the smaller amount of data has to be written per drive so the faster the drives can accomplish this.

RAID 0+1 or 10: This configuration combines two striped RAID 0 drives with two more drives that mirror the first two. This provides most of the speed of the RAID 0 with the data redundancy of the RAID 1.

There are many more types of RAIDs but these are the primary ones you are likely to use and run into in both computers and NAS (Network Attached Storage) devices. Since we are talking about preventing data loss you are best served by using a simple mirroring or RAID 1 configuration. Many computer motherboards and virtually all NAS devices support this configuration. One thing to note is that not all computers support RAIDs, many do, but always check and never assume.

Another nice thing is that with many RAID controllers set up this way if something happens you can pull the drive out and read it on another machine to get your data off of it. Exceptions to this include many of the Dell PERC RAID adapters which use a proprietary method of writing the data which makes it unreadable in other computers.

If purchasing a new motherboard, new computer or RAID controller card I would suggest getting one with an Intel RAID chipset. These will allow you to pull a mirrored drive off and read it in another computer even if that other computer does not have an Intel controller in it. In addition, it will allow you to rebuild (when a drive fails and you replace it, rebuilding is the process of doing the initial copy from one drive to the other) the array in your operating system while using it instead of having to do it in the BIOS before the computer boots. Since this rebuild can take many hours it sure is nice to have a functioning computer while this is going on instead of a doorstop.

NASs, or Network Attached Storage devices are basically small computers which provide file sharing services to your network. They often can also connect to computers via USB. While not providing all the services and capability of a full blown server they can provide almost everything a home and small business user needs in an inexpensive and compact form factor.

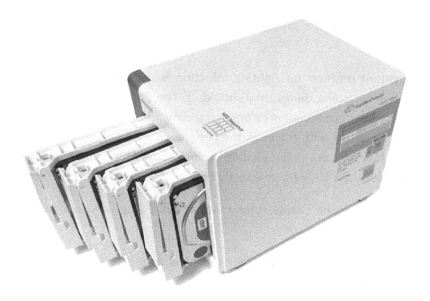

If you want to use a RAID in a NAS instead of directly in your computer, I recommend QNAP devices. They are robust, reliable, reasonably priced and available in a really large variety of models. (I had said "an absolutely huge variety" in that last sentence and changed it to "a really large variety" so I could use a fourth R in the sentence, heh.)

A great reason to use a NAS as your RAID device is so everyone in your home can share it. The down side is the speed is limited to your network speed. I highly discourage you to use your NAS in a wireless network environment unless you are dealing with really small files (keeping your documents, picture and music files would be great) but doing audio editing, video editing or streaming video off of one over wireless if you have more than one person using it could be problematic. This is not an issue with the NAS but with wireless networks in general even considering the faster 802.11ac speeds.

7.3 Virus/Spyware/Crypto prevention

Preventing an infection is always easier than removing and repairing the computer after the fact. If you are old enough you have probably heard "an ounce of prevention is worth a pound of cure" which is just as true here as anywhere else it could be applied.

Stopping infections is a three pronged approach; user control, updates and preventative software.

The most important method for fighting infection is user control which basically means stopping people from doing things they shouldn't. The vast majority of infections I remove are caused by the user not knowing or understanding what they are doing. That isn't saying there is something wrong with the user, the people working to infect your computer are no longer little kids playing a prank but include multi-million dollar corporations with extensive training facilities for their workers on exactly how best to exploit your weaknesses.

Fortunately there are some simple rules that can go a long way towards keeping today's users infection free, these include:

1) Microsoft, Windows, Dell, or any other technical support people will never call you. If someone calls and says they are from some company and that there is a problem with your computer, they are lying. If you let them remote in and show you all the errors in your log files, they are still lying. Errors in the log files are normal on every computer out there. Hang up the phone.

2) If you see something on the screen that tells you there is a problem and that you should call a certain phone number, don't do it. Your computer will not tell you who to call. If in doubt look up that phone number on a search engine such as Yahoo, Google or Bing and the odds are that you will see tons of people telling you it is a scam. If still in doubt, call your local computer company and ask; most will not charge you for a quick question. This includes notices from the police, FBI or IRS.

3) Free software can be anything but free. While there is certainly a lot of high quality free software available on the internet the unfortunate truth is that the overwhelming majority of free screensavers, backgrounds, etc. are all full of some kind of software that you do not

want. The best case is that it can really slow down your computer and cause problems, the worst case is that it will infect you with spyware or even encrypt everything you have.

4) Never open an email attachment that you are not absolutely positive is legitimate. Even if it says it is coming from someplace you do business with, be careful. The majority of crypto infections I see are done this way. A user may get an attachment from their bank and it doesn't dawn on them until after they are infected that their bank doesn't normally send them a PDF attachment. If you are 99.999999999999% sure that is a legitimate attachment, that isn't 100% and you should open it on an IOS or Android tablet before opening it on your computer as those devices so far have proven immune to crypto infection.

5) Install an ad blocker such as AdBlockPlus in your browser. I hate to have to do this because a lot of free content online is paid for by ads, but there are too many infections being spread by ads these days. Besides, many websites use so many ads that it massively slows down anything you try to do. This solves both problems. If you run across a website where you know the owner and want them to get paid you can whitelist that site to allow the ads through, which you may also have to do to be able to read the content on some sites. This is both a software solution and a user control problem so it is listed in both sections.

6) Never give your passwords or credit cards to anyone you do not know, ever. Even if they say they are from some legitimate place, and even if they know some things about you, never ever give out that information. Now if you are online at a retailer such as Amazon.com and they need your information that is fine. This also works hand in hand with item 1 in that you should never give your details out to anyone who calls you, ever.

7) Never click on links in emails. Say you get an email from your bank saying there is a problem with your account and that you need to change your password. Then they provide you with a link to their website to allow you to change it. Wrong! That link probably is not to your bank's website but to a fake website made to look exactly like your bank's. If you think it is a real email, call your bank. This scam applies to banks, PayPal, eBay, Amazon and many other sites.

Next we come to updates which consist of updates for the operating system, drivers and user installed software. This applies equally to any and all platforms including Windows, Mac, Linux, IOS and Android as well as others. Flaws and exploits in software account for a huge amount of infections from virus and spyware authors. Probably the largest single victim is the web browser such as Internet Explorer, Edge, Safari, Chrome and Firefox. These must be kept up to date as soon as a patch comes out.

Operating system patches are generally easy to get and install on most platforms. Windows, Linux and Mac have central points to install updates for those operating systems. In addition all three have facilities to update user installed software if it was done through their installer programs (Windows store, Linux package installer, Mac App Store respectively).

Software downloaded and installed outside of these facilities needs to be manually updated. On Windows a program like Glary Utilities (www.glarysoft.com) has software update checks built in with links to download the updates for some software. While this only covers a small percentage of possible software, it does seem to cover the preponderance of popular software, plugging the bulk of exploits.

Drivers are updated well in Linux and Mac, and not so well in Windows. To keep your drivers current in Windows you are forced to visit a plethora of websites from the various manufacturers, downloading and updating manually. Unless of course you have a program like Driver Booster (www.iobit.com/en/driver-booster.php). This free software (a more advanced version is available for a small fee) will show you all the updates for your hardware, download and install them in one move. Absolutely worth the money as long as you can put up with the few ads it displays.

Updates for IOS and Android are pretty much automatic and you have little to no control over them. With some devices you will get all the updates for the operating system that your device can support regardless of carrier (Apple is great at this). Others depend on carrier and manufacturer such as Samsung always taking longer to get Android updates than Google's own Nexus products, and even other competition such as LG. Just make sure that automatic updates for anything related to the operating system is turned on.

App updates for IOS and Android are handled by the Apple App Store and Google Play Store respectively. Both have the ability to automatically download and install updates in the background. Generally this is a good idea. There are times however when you may not want a specific app to update for compatibility or other reasons, both systems make it easy to update manually so this is not a problem.

Apple devices are all but impervious to attacks however Android is not. The largest current problem with the Android versus IOS devices is Google's lack of control over their Play Store. If they would make the rules regarding submission more stringent and their inspection of submitted apps more rigorous then they would be much more comparable. Instead, you need to be very careful installing apps from the Google Play Store, read the reviews, be wary of any software not published by an established developer or company and be sure to read the fine print.

Now we come to the topic of security software. Security software includes anti-virus software, firewalls, ad blockers, spam blockers and more.

Viruses are much less prevalent today than they were ten years ago and anti-virus software has reflected the change. More and more anti-virus software is becoming anti-spyware software. In addition, a switch from simply rules based detection (where the software has to have been told about a specific infection type in order to detect and remove it) to a more heuristics based system (where the software looks for suspicious behavior) has made them more effective than ever.

Unfortunately spyware writers have become much more sophisticated as well since they are motivated by big money. This tug of war has made both sides very nimble and both advance at a staggering rate.

If you follow the guidelines above for user control and keep your system up to date with patches and fixes in the operating system, drivers and installed software, you technically could do without anti-virus software. The problem is that few people (myself included) are as diligent as they should be on these fronts. This is where the security software provides the last line of defense.

Currently, my two favorite paid antivirus manufacturers are Kaspersky and Norton. For free products I prefer Panda and Avira free editions. Antivirus products vary, sometimes wildly, over time in their effectiveness and usability. Since there is no way I can keep up with all of them there are two websites I use to give me unbiased information to make my choices: av-comparatives.org and av-test.org.

Both of these websites publish reports on the effectiveness of antivirus packages. Some packages may appear on one and not on the other. The biggest names however will appear on both lists. I typically read both at least once a year. You don't have to read all the huge reports, just glance over them and see the scores they provide in their graphs.

I also do not change antivirus packages unless there is a compelling reason. If I am currently using Kaspersky which was ranked on the top out of fifteen packages this year and next year they are ranked number three, I probably won't switch because that drop is not significant enough. All the packages go up and down over time.

Alternately there was a package that the company I work for used to sell that was pretty highly ranked when they sold a bunch of copies. Shortly thereafter it was bought and sold a couple of times and their rankings plummeted. By that I don't mean dropped a few places, I mean from somewhere around fifth place to dead last, below all the free antiviruses.

Watch the trends more than the exact placement. I like Kaspersky for my personal machines because they are consistently in the top three or so on both websites and have been there for years. I am however beginning to switch over to Avira free as it has been scoring at or near the top of the charts for some time now and my initial tests are very positive. If I can save a few bucks a year and get the same level of protection, why not?

When selecting a package you may see different packages by the same manufacturer such as "antivirus" and "internet security". Generally the antivirus or antispyware portion of these are identical while the internet security version adds more features such as a more robust firewall, email antispam (check out the articles on my website at www.paperbirdtek.com for the best free antispam solution), parental controls, etc. Check the manufacturer's website to see what features you want and then choose the package with those features.

Crypto or ransomware threats require a different type of software to help prevent it. We have covered this in more detail previously but I will touch on it again for those who skip around in the book.

On a Windows computer you can download a program called CryptoPrevent. This software was written by Foolish IT and is available from www.foolishit.com. This tool isn't magical, it simply prevents executable programs from running from places it really shouldn't. The majority of ransomware runs this way, so this can stop it before it has a chance to encrypt your files.

The CryptoPrevent basic software is free, with paid versions providing automatic upgrades and more features. If you are seriously worried you may do something stupid, I would suggest you pay for the pro version and make sure it was always up to date.

Bitdefender is an antivirus manufacturer who has released ransomware protection both in their antivirus products and as a standalone free product, Bitdefender Anti-Ransomware (labs.bitdefender.com/2016/03/combination-crypto-ransomware-vaccine-released/). This seems to be a pretty good piece of free software for protection against the CTB-Locker, Locky and TeslaCrypt crypto ransomware families which supposedly includes the popular versions of Cryptolocker.

Another antispyware software vendor, HitmanPro, has released a piece of software called HitmanPro.Alert which says it will not prevent the infection but will prevent the encryption of your data. The software is available from www.surfright.nl and I believe is $24.95 for one year. It is also licensed in a 3 pack and in a 3 year license. Since this solution uses a completely different approach to ransomware protection it could be effectively used in conjunction with CryptoPrevent as a two pronged solution.

One caution: I have heard of a few problems with the HitmanPro solution such as software incompatibilities. Since I do not run the software myself, I would suggest you do a quick internet search just to make sure.

Malwarebytes is working on a new program, Malwarebytes Anti Ransomware or MBARW for short. You cannot currently buy the program or just download it, but there is a beta program you can sign up for. More information is available in their forums at (forums.malwarebytes.org).

No software is a substitute for good ole common sense and backups but it can work well with them to not only keep you out of trouble, but get you out of a jam when everything fails.

Part 8: What if you don't want the data to be recoverable?

There are times when you don't want someone to be able to use a book like this to get the data back. You might have sensitive financial data, have plans for a product you are designing and are going to patent, writing a new recipe for a soft drink that will take the world by storm, be fighting government oppression or any number of other things. You don't have to be doing something nefarious to want data permanently hidden or destroyed.

My biggest call for this type of service is not from terrorists, but from people who are upgrading their computers and simply want to make sure their personal information does not get out into the hands of criminals. Make no mistake, criminals are very sophisticated these days and sift through trash cans, dumpsters, Goodwill stores and flea markets looking for discarded hard drives where they can restore banking and personal information. That often leads to identity theft and major headaches with your bank and credit cards, and even with the IRS.

Even if you are giving your old PC to your best friend for their kid, or your aunt for her web surfing, what happens when they are done with it? What happens if the first thing they do is upgrade the hard drive and throw the old one away? You may trust who you give it to, but how about the people they give it to in turn?

Fortunately securing your information can be pretty easy and straight forward.

8.1 Encryption

Encryption allows you to hide or obfuscate your data. When it is encrypted, no one can read it or even tell what it is. You can encrypt one file, a folder or an entire hard drive. The only way to access the data is to enter the key (password or passphrase).

Encryption comes in a variety of types and strengths. Common types of encryption include AES, Blowfish and 3DES. Key strengths come 32bit to 448bit standards. Let's look into what this all means.

The type of encryption refers to the mathematical process of encrypting and decrypting the data. Over the years people have developed different and more robust mathematical formulas to use in encryption. In the three we are discussing DES (the base of 3DES) was created in 1975, Blowfish in 1993 while both 3DES and AES appeared in 1998.

Each type of encryption has advantages and disadvantages but all three are secure enough for most people. AES is probably the most secure and is currently used by many governments including Canada and the United States for up to top secret documents. 3DES is widely used by the electronic payment industry and in many Microsoft products.

Key strengths refers to the length of the key in bits. The more bits, the more difficult it is to mathematically crack the key.

Brute force attacks attempt to guess your password by entering passwords over and over at a very high speed. There are two different basic types of attacks like this, dictionary and non-dictionary. Dictionary attacks go through words in the dictionary looking for a match while non-dictionary may use sequential (0, 1, 2, 3, etc) or random data. Non-dictionary attacks take far longer than dictionary.

When selecting your password it is best to use a long random password which contains both upper and lower case letters, numbers and symbols ("E8&b!21z$Y..awD1+c@Q" would be an excellent password). Be sure not to write down your password.

You should also be careful with password apps that store your passwords electronically on your computer or phone. The problem I have seen with some people is that they will use very complex passwords for their online banking and then store that excellent password in a password program with a very simple password protecting it. This means that if someone guesses or cracks the easy password on their password storage program, they now have access to all the person's very strong passwords without having to crack them. DOH!

Encrypting your data these days is pretty easy. If you own an IOS device, it already is. Windows Vista & Windows 7 Ultimate and Enterprise editions or Windows 8+ Professional & Enterprise editions as well as Windows 10 have BitLocker drive encryption built in. Macs include FileVault encryption in MacOS 10.7 and later and have an even more robust encryption scheme in MacOS Sierra. Android devices also include the option to encrypt everything although I have not seen it enabled by default yet like on IOS devices, so you may have to flip a switch yourself. Linux of course has encryption built in as well.

So what if you have an older version of Windows or an unsupported version like Windows Home that does not include BitLocker?

A free solution is DiskCrypter available from DiskCryptor.net. This is an open source solution which looks pretty good but has not been updated since 2014 (as of mid 2016).

If you are willing to pay real money for your encryption, Norton has their encryption for $119 or you could upgrade from Windows 10 Home to Windows 10 Pro for $99 and use Bitlocker. I would personally just upgrade Windows as Bitlocker will obviously be the best integrated directly into Windows.

8.2 Data destruction

The easiest way to destroy data on a hard drive is to simply drill one or more holes completely through the drive and all the platters. This does not technically destroy much of the data but it does prevent it from being read without an awful large amount of time, effort and special equipment. If you are keeping your personal identity and banking information safe, this is more than enough. If you are hiding something that a government may want, you may need to do a little more.

While drilling holes is fast, easy and fairly effective it also destroys the hard drive. This may be fine if you are getting rid of the computer and you do this before putting it in your local dump's electronics pile. It will not be very nice if you want to keep using the computer.

The next option which is both less physically destructive and more effective, yet takes far longer to accomplish, is a disk wipe. Unlike just deleting data on the drive, formatting or repartitioning, a disk wipe actually writes something to every single sector on the hard drive. This could be as simple (yet still fairly effective) as writing a "0" to every bit on the drive. It could also be much more effective if it made multiple passes and even more effective if you replace the "0" with random data.

The more effective the disk wipe, the longer it will take. It takes quite a while to completely fill every single bit available on a hard drive, and even more when you need to overwrite each bit multiple times. Fortunately there are programs out there that will do it for us.

The good news is that with the density of data on hard drives these days a simple single pass of writing zeros to every bit on the drive is far more secure than it was ten years ago. It is now incredibly difficult for even governments to recover data that has been overwritten once.

My favorite program for this for years has been Active Killdisk (www.killdisk.com). This was always a DOS based program and many people still use the DOS version (it is still included on UBCD for example). Their new version is for Windows and Linux and both have free versions you can download. These free versions are limited in several ways however they will do single pass zero writing to virtually any drive including drives over 4TB in size.

If you are overthrowing an oppressive government you may want something even more secure and purchasing their professional version for $40 which among other things offers more than 20 international erasing standards plus a User Defined method.

Mac users have it made as you can simply boot to your DVD/USB/Recovery partition and run the included Disk Utility program. Select your hard drive (not the recovery drive), select the erase tab, select Mac OS Extended (Journaled), click on Security Options button and then pick which method of deletion (up to 32 passes!) you wish to use.

If you have an Android device that you want to securely delete data from you should take a look at iShredder (www.protectstar.com). This excellent free app can not only do simple zero overwrites but also DoD 5220.22-M ECE. For under $6 you can get the enterprise version which has more data wiping algorithms and supports wiping SMS, texts, contacts and much more.

For IOS users, all phones after about the 3GS are encrypted so once you use the built in ability to delete all data and settings in the settings menu all that the phone has to do is delete the key used to encrypt and decrypt the information and it is in effect all securely wiped. No apps are needed.

SSDs are a different animal entirely. Engineers at the University of California published a paper which they have made available online for anyone to download and read at www.usenix.org/legacy/events/fast11/tech/full_papers/Wei.pdf. This paper talks about the difficulties in securely erasing data from SSDs given the way SSDs store the data. This is made even more difficult because most machines with SSDs use TRIM (a method of dealing with deleted files and sectors which dramatically reduces the overhead needed to process these types of commands) which further obfuscates where the data truly is.

The only reliable solution (other than physical destruction of the drive) is for the data on the drive to have been encrypted and then delete the encryption key, exactly what Apple does on their IOS devices. Overwriting of every available sector on these drives could take hundreds of hours and/or substantially reduce the lifecycle of the drive given that SSDs are rated to a certain number of writes.

Part 9: Wrapping up

I hope that I have covered enough for the typical end user to recover some or all of their data, and for the budding recovery technician to get a firm grasp on the subject. There are so many variables and possibilities in this field that one could write ten books this size and never get close to all the scenarios you could encounter. It was never my intent to cover them all.

That being said this book has grown larger than I ever expected. What started out as maybe a hundred page booklet at most, has grown to be over twice that size and there was a lot of things I removed as being just too much information for this little primer.

What follows are supplements that I hope will help you use this book and show you where to go when you have outgrown it.

Good luck!

9.1 Talking with the customer

For many budding technicians the hardest part of the job is not repairing the computer, it is dealing with the customer. I know several techs who are great with the technology but are horrible with people. I also know techs who are great with people but can't fix a computer whose only problem is it isn't plugged into power.

The first rule is, do not lie to a customer. As long as you stick to this rule everything else is a lot easier. This does not necessarily mean you have to tell them everything, just don't tell them anything untrue. Sometimes providing too much information is a problem in itself that we will talk about in a little while.

This also works for things they could perceive as a lie, or stretching the truth. For example I try to never tell a customer I will get their data back, I always try to tell them there is a good chance, so so chance or a bad chance they will get any data back. I also say that I will do my best but sometimes there is just nothing I can do.

The next rule is to keep it simple. Typical customers do not know a spindle from a platter, and don't care to. Break down what you need to tell them into something they can understand. Try to use analogies that relate to something the customer is familiar with. You could of course use the record player to talk about a hard drive if you think the person is either old enough, or into music enough to get that analogy. You can also use car tires as an effective analogy.

Be careful here, try not to over simplify things too much. You can always start the conversation with something like "If I get too simple or too technical just stop me and let me know" and proceed from there. This at least lets them know you are trying to make it work for them and they will appreciate it.

This is typically where I start to explain the options the customer has such as letting me work on it or sending it off to be recovered by a recovery specialist. One thing I make clear to the customer is that there is a chance, although in my opinion only a small one, that my recovery actions may hamper the efforts of a specialist even to the point of making something they could have recovered impossible to recover. I do not think this has ever happened however I want that warning out there just in case.

While explaining things to the customer you need to take all the information you have and distill the overall idea into something that not only the customer can understand as we previously talked about, but that is short and to the point. Customers can easily get overwhelmed with too much information. Here is the layout of what I try to tell my customer:

1) The current state of the equipment they brought in such as "your hard drive will not boot but I can still see that there is data on it"
2) The likelihood that I can get anything off such as "Since I can see data on there, there is a fairly good chance I can get some of that data off"
3) Then the warnings like "Of course if I try there is a very small chance that could make things worse should we need to send the drive to a specialist"
4) Now I explain about the specialist like "sending a drive to a specialist is safer and more likely to result in getting all your data back, however it can easily cost over a thousand dollars. Is that an option you would like to explore?"
5) Next is always the same question, what caused it? I almost always have the same answer, that I have no idea however it could have been lightning, a fault in the drive, an impact, etc etc.
6) Lastly you always ask the customer if they have any other questions or concerns.

Other things you may want to work into the conversation are things like if there are any particular files they really need. I have had customers come in after one or two files they "had" to have and the rest would be nice but not required. Always make sure that you know exactly what you are going after and make sure the customer is aware that you are primarily seeking this particular thing.

Once you get data back you should always make a backup of everything you recovered. You would be amazed at the places people store their files so do not assume that just because you would never ever put your important documents in the recycle bin as a storage option that someone else would not.

Now we call the customer to come in and look at the files you have recovered and ask them to verify that these are indeed what they wanted. This is also the time to approach them about how they want the files delivered.

If we are talking about a couple of small files they may just want them emailed to them or put on a USB drive they provide.

If there are a lot of files then they may want them put on a large USB drive or an external USB hard drive.

You may have recovered the entire system in which case you could copy the clone to another hard drive and have their computer booting right up to where it was before there was a problem. If this is the case and if they do not have a massive amount of data see if they might be interested in an SSD instead of a hard drive.

After all of this is done and they are getting ready to pick up their data and pay you is the right time to suggest options for backing up their data so this does not happen again. You need to be careful how you word it because even though we know it was their fault for not backing it up last time telling them that is a sure fire way to lose the customer.

Start off the conversation with something like "Would you like me to show you some easy and inexpensive new ways to back up your data to help prevent future issues from hardware failures and virus infections?"

This sentence implies that there are "new" ways that might work whereas the old ones they surely looked into just didn't work for them. It also implies it was the fault of the hardware for failing, or the virus for infecting their system, not their fault for not backing things up.

So what happens when things don't work as they should, you fail to get back what they want or anything at all? Most of the time nothing spectacular. You tell them you did everything you could but that the damage was just too great. You tell them you are sorry the data could not be recovered. You bill them for your time and everyone leaves amicably.

Every once in a great while this doesn't work, the shouting starts and things get heated. When this happens there are some rules you need to stick with:

1) Never raise your voice. Not even a little. You need to be the calm one regardless of what they do.

2) Never use profanity even if they do. In fact, even if this is someone you grew up with and have known for thirty years, no profanity.

3) Stand your ground. If they advance, stay right where you are. If they get so close that you are uncomfortable with it ask them politely to move back or you will have to call security/the police. The reason for this is that people who start screaming because you couldn't do something you warned them might not work are looking to intimidate you into something such as paying to have it recovered by a specialist. If you start backing away or cowering they will know they can intimidate you. The exception here is if you are in their home or a business where you feel confined then you should leave. If they prevent you from leaving dial 911 immediately.

4) If you are working for someone else, make sure you immediately offer to allow them to speak to a manager. Managers should in theory have experience and training on dealing with unreasonable customers and this will take the load off of you and make the customer feel their problem is important enough to get a manager's attention.

5) Stand by your statements, your quotes and your decisions. Nothing will make this worse than if you start backtracking or giving things away. Offering discounts is often seen as admitting you did something wrong.

It is an unfortunate part of life these days that there are just some people you will not be able to please. I personally have had to have someone removed from my home by police after they followed me home from the office. I was not even the technician who worked on their equipment but the manager who got brought in to try to calm them down. Only calling the police and having them physically removed accomplished that.

Generally speaking though, being truthful, respectful, polite and professional will get you through 99.99% of anything you run into.

9.2 Where to go from here

Assuming this book has piqued your interest, you might want to go further and learn more. If that's the case you can use the following information to expand your data recovery skill set. If you find something particularly useful that is not on this list take a minute to let me know so I can update it for future versions of this book.

Online forums-

HDDGuru Forums (forum.hddguru.com)

EaseUS Forums (forum.easeus.com)

Data Medics (www.data-medics.com/forum/)

Books -

Pro Data Backup and Recovery by Steven Nelson

The Basics of Digital Forensics: The Primer for Getting Started in Digital Forensics by John Sammons

Data Recovery: Ensuring Data Availability by Preston de Guise

Training –

My Hard Drive Died (www.myharddrivedied.com/data-recovery-training)

DeepSpar Data Recovery Systems (www.deepspar.com/training-product-training.html)

9.3 Index

9.4 Glossary

3DES – A method where the Data Encryption Standard algorithm is used three times to encrypt a piece of data. Originally developed in 1998 this currently is not as popular as AES encryption.

4k TV – A television set that displays content at a resolution of 3840 x 2160 or 4096 x 2160. This is considered the next standard after 1080p which had a resolution of 1920x1080. Keep in mind that this is just a piece of the puzzle when determining the picture quality of a television. Other factors include (but are not limited to) things such as black levels, maximum brightness levels, off axis viewing, and dynamic range.

Ad Blocker – A browser plugin or piece of software that primarily filters web pages to block out advertisements that would normally be present on the pages. They may also block pop-ups and text advertisements such as Google AdWords. These are used mainly to speed up page load times, reduce distractions and reduce the risk of infection from hijacked ads or websites.

Advanced Encryption Standard - Developed in 1998 the Advanced Encryption Standard is one of the most popular encryption methods today.

AES – See Advanced Encryption Standard.

Allocation Block – In a Macintosh's HFS+ file system each volume is divided into sectors of 512 bytes and then these sectors are grouped into allocation blocks. Each allocation block can contain one or more sectors.

Allocation File – A file that lists all allocation blocks on the drive along with a 0 if the block is available/empty or a 1 if it is currently in use on Macintosh HFS+ drives.

Anti-Static Mat – A type of mat you place on a workbench and then put electronic parts on top of. These are designed to ground any static that may build up on the worker or parts. These mats are grounded via a wire typically plugged into a grounded electrical outlet.

Anti-Static Wrist Strap – A strap that goes around a person's wrist that has a wire which runs to ground. This will ground any static electricity that may build up so that it does not harm an electronic device the person may touch.

Antivirus – Software that is designed to prevent the infection and facilitate the removal of viruses.

Antispyware– Software that is designed to prevent the infection and facilitate the removal of spyware.

APFS – See Apple File System.

App Store – Generally refers to the store hosted by Apple that contains Apps which are either for sale or free for the user to download. This App Store has an app which is included on all Apple devices including iPhones, iPads, iPods and Mac computers.

Apple File System – A new method of storing files on the hard drive or SSD of a Mac computer. This file system was first introduced in MacOS Sierra in 2016 although the file system was still considered to be in beta and was not the default file system for Sierra installation or operation.

Areal Density – The density at which data is packed onto a hard drive usually measured in BPSI or Bits Per Square Inch. The higher the areal density the more data can be stored in a given amount of area and the faster that data can be read, all other things being equal.

Arm – The arm is the part of the hard drive which supports the reading/writing head over the spinning platters. This is very similar in functionality to the tone arm on a turntable.

Attach – Connecting one device to another. You can connect a hard drive to a computer and it is said to be attached. This can be either physically connected with wires, screws, etc. or it can also mean to logically attach something such as importing foreign file systems using software.

Author – The person or persons who wrote, modified and/or published a given piece of software.

Backup – A second copy of data which is not being used. Moving data from your hard drive to an external device sold as a backup device does not make a backup, that is simply the same data moved. Data must have at least two copies, one of which is not in use, in order to be considered to have a backup copy.

Basic Disk Type – The default type of NTFS partition that is limited to a maximum of four partitions using MBR or 128 using GPT. They also cannot create software based RAID or use partitions that span across multiple hard drives.

Basic Input Output System – Software that is typically on a single chip on something like a motherboard that does very basic control of the hardware, enough so that it can hand off control to a computer operating system. Without this a computer would not be able to boot to Windows, MacOS or Linux.

BD – See Blu-Ray Disc.

Bench Machine – Usually a desktop type computer dedicated to use on a computer technician's workbench for operations where a computer other than the one being worked on is required. Examples for use include cloning drives, virus scans, data recovery and diagnostics.

BIOS – See Basic Input Output Statement

Bit – A single piece of digitally stored information represented by either a 0 or a 1. It is sometimes also referred to as either off or on.

Bit Clone – The act of copying one storage device to another one bit at a time regardless of file system, operating system or what may or may not be on that part of the device. It copies empty sectors as well as sectors with data on them.

Bits Per Square Inch – The measurement used to define the areal density of a hard drive platter.

Blowfish – An encryption algorithm that was developed in 1993 to replace DES. While a pretty robust encryption method, it is generally less popular than AES.

Blu-Ray Disc - An optical disc designed to replace the DVD that movies came on and DVD data discs that software came on. A single layer stores 25GB while one with dual layers stores 50GB. Newer standards include discs with 100GB or more in capacity. This allows for not only high resolution video (even better than what can be streamed today) but also usually contains lossless multichannel audio which is virtually impossible to stream.

Board – See Circuit Board.

Boot – The process of initializing a computer system so that it is ready for operation. The boot process typically checks the hardware in a system, then loads a piece of software that in turn allows the operating system to load and run.

Boot up – The process of booting. See Boot.

BPSI – See Bits Per Square Inch.

Bug – A defect or error in software.

Business Use – Typically refers to something such as software being used for a purpose or in support of a purpose that entails making a profit. The specific use does not have to generate a profit, but if it supports another thing that does earn a profit that would be considered business use. For example software used to type phone messages may not actually generate money (you don't get paid for each message you take) but taking the messages is an integral part to the operation of the business, so it is for business use.

Byte – Eight bits of data.

Cache – Cache is a place where information is stored before it is used, usually in a faster place than the final destination. For example hard drives typically have cache on them as a small amount of fast memory which acts as a temporary holding area. This allows the computer to dump data to the hard drive cache extremely quickly and move on to other tasks allowing the cache to write that data to the hard drive without the need for the computer to wait. The water in your hot water heater could be said to work the same way; water is heated in the tank and waits to be sent to you so you do not have to wait while it is heated.

Capacitor – An electronic component that stores electricity and can use it as a buffer. These devices can contain a liquid which can overheat and cause the metal casing of the capacitor to bulge and even start to leak fluid onto the surrounding components or board. Swollen or leaking capacitors can often cause erratic behavior or complete failure of an electronic device.

Card Reader – A device used to read memory cards typically found in devices such as cameras. These readers can be built into a computer or device, or be external connecting primarily via USB.

Carrier – The company that provides cellular service to a device such as a phone, tablet or portable hotspot/MIFI device. These providers include companies in the US such as Verizon, ATT, Sprint, and T-Mobile.

Catalog File - The Catalog File contains the information on where every file and directory on the volume is located along with other file related information. This is basically a large database file.

CD – See Compact Disc

CDROM – Stands for Compact Disc Read Only Memory and is a type of compact disc that can only be read and not written to.

CDR - Stands for Compact Disc Recordable and is a type of compact disc that the end user can write to once and read multiple times.

CDRW – Stands for Compact Disc Re-Writable and is a type of compact disc that the end user can read, erase and write to multiple times.

Ceramic – A substance that is inorganic and non-metallic such as clay. Examples include typical dishes, bricks, clay pots, sinks and toilets.

CF – See Compact Flash.

Chip – See Microchip.

Chromebook – A type of computer (usually a laptop) that runs the Chrome operating system from Google which is a derivative of Linux. These computers are known for being inexpensive and robust but lack the ability to run mainstream installable software such as Photoshop or QuickBooks. Instead these run software located online in the installed Chrome web browser.

CHS – See Cylinder Head Sector.

Circuit Board - Generally a piece of plastic that has electronic components on them. These components may be connected with wires, traces (paths of conductive material) or by directly touching another component. These components are what make electronic devices work.

Clean Room – A virtually air-tight room where special equipment removes almost all possible particles and contaminates from the air so that opening devices such as hard drives is possible. Very stringent controls and regulations are usually in place on what can and cannot be brought into the room as well (clothing/shoes/hair must be covered, no animals allowed, no purses or bags, etc.) to help prevent contamination.

Clone – Term used for the process or result of making an exact copy of a hard drive or other media. You can clone a drive (the act of making the copy) or you can have a clone of a drive (the resultant copy of the process). This is very similar to the often used term Xerox which can apply to making a copy of a piece of paper or the resultant copy.

Clones (APFS) – A feature of the new Apple File System introduced in MacOS Sierra. This provides Windows shadow copy like functionality with a twist. Instead of just keeping multiple copies of a file it keeps the original and then different files which only contain the changes. This makes storing multiple versions of a file take up less space and make the copying process much faster.

Cloud – Refers to a place or places on the internet where data, programs or media can be stored. Items stored here are said to be "in the cloud". These places are different than standard servers in that part or all of the data being stored is usually stored in multiple locations.

Cloud Backup – A backup solution where your information is backed up to the cloud instead of to media in your immediate control.

Cluster – The smallest area of a storage device that an operating system can address is a single cluster. Clusters are made up of one or more sectors, the smallest division of a hard drive.

Command – A statement that tells a computer or program what to do.

Command Prompt – On a DOS or Windows computer it is a program that allows you to directly type commands to the operating system without using a mouse or graphics of any kind.

Commercial Use – Generally refers to software being used to generate money, or by an entity whose job it is to generate income. Keeping a shopping list for your home is not commercial use, keeping the exact same list with the exact same items on it for your office is commercial use. Also, if you are paid in any way (including bartering) for something that the software had any part whatsoever in creating or assisting in, then that is commercial use.

Compact Disc – An optical media that can hold audio, or data (CDROM, CDR and CDRW). These plastic discs use variances in reflectivity as read by a drive using a laser beam to transfer digital 0s and 1s as data.

Compact Flash – A type of memory card used in higher end cameras and some media players. Originally designed for higher transfer speeds and greater storage capacity than alternatives such as SD.

Compression – Can reduce the size of a piece of data. Can be achieved by several methods generally by replacing patterns with markers. For example if you have a number 11213981164811 you could compress it by saying that 11=a and then making the number a21398a648a making the data three digits smaller. Another program can then reverse this procedure to decompress the data back to its original state.

Computer – A device used to view, store and manipulate data. In this book this refers to a desktop or laptop computer running a standard operating system such as Windows, MacOS or Linux. It technically also includes devices such as smartphones and tablets.

Controller – A device that provides commands and controls for other devices. Examples include hard drive controllers which interface with computer motherboards and provide connections where the hard drives can be plugged in. These controllers may be built in to the motherboard or may be cards which then plug into a slot on the motherboard or even into an external interface such as a USB port.

Corrupt – When data is not as it is intended then it is said to be corrupt. For example if you were to type the alphabet correctly on the keyboard and it showed on the screen as "abc4fghi*@nnpqrst%vxwyz" then that data would be considered corrupt.

CMD – Stands for Command and is used in Windows computers to launch a command prompt where typed commands can be issued directly to the operating system.

CRC – See Cyclic Redundancy Check.

Crypto – A shorthand term for either Cryptography or the Cryptolocker virus. Often the term crypto is used to refer to any software that encrypts your files (Cryptolocker is only one such virus).

Cryptography – The scientific field of encrypting data.

Cryptolocker – A particular virus that encrypts a user's files and forces them to pay money to get them decrypted so that they are usable again.

Cyclic Redundancy Check – A number generated mathematically based on the data in a file. This number is then used to verify the integrity of the data file once it has been transmitted. If the original CRC number differs from the number generated after a file has been transmitted, that infers the data is either corrupt or has been tampered with and should not be used.

Cylinder - A logical grouping of tracks on the hard drive platters used in addressing.

Cylinder Head Sector – A method of addressing a specific location on a hard drive.

Data – I use the term data to refer to your documents, settings, music, videos etc. This is distinct from the programs used to create the data. For example Microsoft Word is a program however any documents created with it is considered data. Microsoft Windows is considered a program but the log files it writes is considered data.

Data Recovery – The act of restoring data to a usable state. This includes undeleting files, copying data off of failed/failing media, restoring data from backups, etc.

Data Wipe – A process used to remove all recoverable traces of data from a device. Once a successful wipe is carried out data recovery is no longer possible except through restoring data from backup located on a different device. Often used to protect financial and personal data before donating or throwing away an old device or computer.

Dead – From the point of view of a technician, a device or computer is "dead" when you attempt to turn it on and absolutely nothing happens. If a light, fan or indicator of any kind activates then the device is not "dead". A good example would be if you had a standard incandescent lamp and did not plug it into the wall, and then turned on the power switch. This is a very important distinction when talking to a technician about your problem.

Decrypt – The process of reversing the encryption process to return the original data back to a usable state.

Desolder – The process of melting the solder and removing it from an electronic component. This is commonly done with a soldering iron and either a solder bulb or wick but can also be done by a specialized desoldering station.

Device – For the purposes of this book a device typically refers to a computer that is neither a traditional desktop nor laptop. This would include smartphones, tablets, media players, media streamers, in-car infotainment systems, LCD photo frames, many new television sets, etc. It can also be used in conjunction with a use such as the term "storage device" meaning virtually anything you can store data on (hard drive, USB drive, floppy disk, CDROM, etc.).

Diagnostics – Can refer to either tools used to diagnose a problem or the actual act of diagnosing a problem. For example I may use hard drive diagnostic software (the tool) to test a hard drive or I may just see how it is behaving and know from experience (the act) what is wrong.

Dictionary Attack – A method of attempting to guess a password by entering all the words in the dictionary, one word at a time.

Digital – Data on computers is stored in a digital format meaning either a one or a zero. This can also be represented by an electronic state of either on or off respectively. Either way there are only two possible states for each piece of data.

Digital Versatile Disc – An optical disc designed to replace the VHS tape that movies came on, the CDROMs we used to store data and possibly (although it failed to do this) the CDs we listened to audio on (the DVD-A was a higher fidelity disc than the CD was). A single layer stored 4.7GB while one with dual layers stored 8.5GB.

Directory – A logical storage container in a file system. This can be thought of as a file folder inside a filing cabinet.

Disc – Refers to optical discs.

Disk – Refers to non-optical disks.

Disk Operating System – The operating system used on the IBM compatible PCs designed to be used off of disks. Originally these were floppy disks and that led to hard drives.

Disk Quota – A system or setting that allows a certain area such as a folder or directory to only contain a certain amount of data. Once that amount of data has been reached and you try to write more data to that area the quota is said to have been exceeded and the write will not be allowed. This keeps users from filling up a storage device.

Disk Wipe – See Data Wipe

DLT Tape – Digital Linear Tape system was a high capacity and high speed system used primarily for data backup. Originally created in 1984 it survived through the early 2000s in capacities up to 800GB.

DOS – See Disk Operating System

Drive – A term used to refer to a storage device.

Drive Letter – In DOS and Windows, mounted storage devices with a partition and formatted file system are given drive letters starting with A and ending with Z. A and B are generally reserved for floppy drives whereas C is usually reserved for the primary boot drive in the machine that contains the operating system. All other drive letters are handed out on a first come, first serve basis.

Driver – A piece of software that works with an operating system to allow a piece of hardware to work. Drivers are used to support sound cards, printers, video cards, your mouse and keyboard and virtually every component in a computer or device.

Dual Layer – Refers to optical discs which have two different layers of reflective material in them. One layer is completely reflective and the other is semi-transparent. The device reading the disc can refocus the laser used to read the media on one layer or the other and thereby read one layer or the other. This allows the disc to store substantially more data although not double as you might think.

Dynamic Disk Type - The more advanced type of NTFS partition that exceed four partitions using MBR or 128 using GPT. These also can create software based RAIDs and use partitions that span across multiple hard drives.

Dynamic Range – In imaging and video it is the range between the darkest dark and lightest light that can be represented. In audio it is the range of frequencies between the lowest and highest that can be reproduced.

DVD – See Digital Versatile Disc.

DVD-R / DVD+R - A format of DVD designed to be written to once by the end user. It used a special dye that when hit with the correct wavelength and power of laser would change reflectivity allowing a different wavelength and power of laser to read those changes as the pits and lands associated with DVD data. This process could only be done once and was irreversible. DVD-R competed with DVD+R format and was generally seen as the more compatible of the two formats.

DVD-RW / DVD+RW – A format of DVD designed to be written to and erased multiple times by the end user. It used a special dye that when hit with the correct wavelength and power of laser would change reflectivity allowing a different wavelength and power of laser to read those changes as the pits and lands associated with DVD data. This process could be repeated over and over during the disc's lifetime. DVD-RW competed with DVD+RW format and was generally seen as the more compatible of the two formats.

Earth Ground – Earth ground refers to something that has a direct current path into the ground. A wire connected to a rod that has been buried in the ground is said to be an earth ground. You could also connect a wire to a metal water pipe that runs underground to gain an earth ground. Do NOT use a gas pipe!

ECC – See Error Correcting Code.

Electro Static Discharge – The static that can be built up through friction such as walking across carpet, sliding clothing across other clothing, moving plastics against each other, etc. Examples are when you touch a metal object after walking across carpet, your hair standing on end after taking off a sweater or how Styrofoam cups stick to plastic wrappers after being removed from the stack. ESD can be very harmful to electronic components.

Encryption – The process of making something unreadable or secret usually done by transposing letters, words or digital information in some manner using mathematical equations.

Encryption Chip – A computer chip that encrypts all data going to and from a device automatically. These are often found in devices such as external hard drives and smartphones.

Error Correcting Code - Refers to hardware or software that watches the data stream in some form for corrupt or incorrect data and has the capability to either correct the problem itself or to request that the data be resent until the error condition no longer exists.

ESD – See Electro Static Discharge.

Execute / Execution – The process of a computing device performing the instructions given to it. If you tell a child to take out the trash that is the instruction, when the child performs that action they could be said to be executing the instructions.

EXT ext2/ext3/ext4 – EXT is the filesystem used by Linux operating systems. The number after the name denotes the version of the filesystem being used. Ext4 is the most current version as of this writing.

Extents – In the Linux ext4 file system small 4k blocks are arranged into contiguous 128MB sections called extents. These extents help reduce fragmentation and also reduce slack.

External Hard Drive – A hard disk drive designed to be used outside a computer or device usually connected using one or more cables (USB, Thunderbolt, ESATA, etc.) but can also be connected wirelessly.

Faraday's Law – Describes the way changing magnetic fields can induce electrical current in a coil, and how the reverse also happens. In a magnetic storage device the read head flies over the platters storing the information. As the magnetic poles change on the platter this induces current which the drive reads as data.

FAT – See File Allocation Table.

FDD – See Floppy Disk Drive.

File – A single instance of data on a storage device. This would be analogous to a single written letter to someone, a single receipt from the store or a single picture.

File Allocation Table – The file system used by DOS and earlier versions of Windows, as well as being popular on removable media such as USB drives. It is very flexible and scalable to a point but cannot match the performance, reliability and sizes of modern filesystems such as NTFS, APFS and ext4.

File System – A method of organizing data on a storage device in such a way that data can be written to and read from the device.

Firmware – Software that is used to make a piece of hardware work at a low level. Firmware is usually stored on a single chip such as in the case of most computer BIOS chips but could also be stored on a storage device such as a flash drive. Firmware is much like an operating system for less complex devices.

Flash Storage – A storage medium where data is stored on memory modules which does not have any moving parts. Flash storage also usually requires no power to retain the information.

Floppy Drive / Floppy Disk Drive – A drive used to read and write to disks where the material being written to were in fact floppy. Disks such as this came in sizes such as 12", 8", 5.25" and 3.5" and were phased out of general use by the year 2000.

Format / Formatting – To format a disk or other media means to write the data to the device that is required for the operation of the file system. This can be tables that will eventually contain the names of the files, where they are stored, etc. and may also contain markers as to where the data portion of the device starts and ends.

Fragmentation – When a file is written to a device such as a hard drive it is written one file after the next. If three files of 4k each are written to the drive one after another, that takes up three consecutive 4k blocks in a row. If you then delete file two and write a 5k file the file system will write 4k of the five in between files 1 and 3 where file 2 had been, then put the extra 1k of that new file after the end of file 3. This splitting of files is called fragmentation.

Full Clone – See Bit Clone.

Glass Master – A process using an actual glass disc to mass replicate optical discs such as CDs.

Globally Unique Identifier – A unique long alphanumeric string used to identify a specific device.

Globally Unique Identifier Partition – See GUID Partition Type.

GPT – See GUID Partition Type.

Grounded / Grounding – An object is said to be grounded when it is connected to the negative side of a DC circuit (such as a device that runs off battery power) or when it is connected to an earth ground (in daily use or with AC circuits).

GUID – See Globally Unique Identifier.

GUID Partition Type – A replacement for the master boot record configuration of storage devices such as hard drives. This configuration information includes the GUID of the storage device, partition information, and file system information. These allow partitions larger than 2TB.

Hack / Hacked – To hack something is to make it do something it was not designed to do. Hacking is not necessarily bad.

Hard Disk Drive / Hard Drive – A device composed of ridged platter(s) that spin around a spindle allowing a movable head to read and write data off of and to the surface of the platter.

Hardware – Physical items. A computer, a chip, a hard drive are all examples of hardware.

Head – A device suspended on the end of an arm that reads and sometimes writes data to media. Heads that both read and write are found in hard drives while heads that only read are found in CDROM drives.

HDD – See Hard Disk Drive.

Hierarchical - Refers to the way some file systems are built in that they have a root which has containers and files, those containers may have more containers and files inside them, and so on. On a typical Windows computer you may have the Windows directory in the root, and then the System32 directory inside that and the Drivers directory inside that. You could represent that by saying C:\Windows\System32\Drivers showing the hierarchy.

HFS / HFS+ - The primary file system used in Macintosh computers today.

IDE – See Integrated Drive Electronics.

Image – A single file that contains all the data necessary to recreate an entire piece of media (a hard drive, optical disc, flash drive, etc.) complete with all data, operating system and information required to make it bootable.

Infected – Refers to software running on a device such as a computer that was not intended by the manufacturer or end user. This can include viruses, spyware, malware, or simply PUPs.

Inode –In the Linux ext file system, data is stored in blocks which are organized into extents, these are then grouped into a maximum of four extents per file making up an inode. Should a file require more than an inode (more than a 512MB file) then the rest of the file is stored in a tree.

Integrated Drive Electronics – A type of interface popular in computers for connecting hard drives and optical drives to motherboards and controller cards from the late 1980s through the early 2000s.

Interface – Refers to what something interacts with. For example the steering wheel and pedals in a car are the driver's interface with the car. The part of software that you see and click on is the software's interface. Cables plug into components in a computer using an interface.

Internal Hard Drive – A type of hard drive designed to operate inside the case of a computer, either a desktop or laptop.

iSesamo – A brand name tool used to open electronic devices such as tablets and smartphones.

ISO – An image of an optical disc such as a CDROM, DVDROM etc.

Jazz Drive – A type of external hard drive where the platters were stored in removable cartridges while the heads remained in the drive. This allowed for large amounts of storage to be accessed quickly. These were available for both Mac and Windows computers.

Jump Drive - A name for a small portable USB flash storage device. Sometimes called a thumb drive.

Key – Refers to the secret or password used to encrypt or decrypt data.

Kindle – A tablet device designed specifically for reading electronic books sold by Amazon. These use specialized screens that are much easier to read than standard tablets but they also lack the additional functionality that other tablets offer.

Kindle Fire – A standard tablet with similar capabilities to other Android tablets and sold by Amazon. Unlike the standard Kindle these are no easier for reading than any other handheld tablet.

LBA – See Logical Block Addressing.

Land – The raised portion of an optical disc's data surface.

Link – A piece of code that when clicked on takes you to an internet web site to view a page or download a file. This code can be on a web page, in an email or in a program on your computer.

Linux – An operating system (like Windows or MacOS) originally written by Linus Torvalds in 1991 as a Unix type system replacement. It currently runs on a wide array of computers and devices including being the basis for Android, ChromeOS and many others.

Logic Board – A board which has electronic components on it in such a manner that it can perform a task based on input given to it. This input is then processed and the board determines the correct course of action.

Logical – In this book it generally refers to a non-physical division of media. For example a piece of paper is a physical media. Dividing the page into sections by drawing lines on it is a logical division whereas tearing it in half to create two pieces of paper is a physical division.

Logical Block Addressing – A method of addressing the space on a hard drive that allows for larger hard drives than the computer could normally use. This basically tricks the computer into thinking the hard drive is smaller than it really is, thereby allowing the use of larger drives.

Logs – Data files that contain information on what is happening, typically used for troubleshooting errors.

Mac – See Macintosh.

Macintosh – A desktop or laptop computer manufactured by Apple Inc.

MacOS - The operating system used by Macintosh computers.

Magnetic Media – Storage media that requires the use of magnets to read and/or require reading the magnetic field or polarity of a certain part as data. Examples include hard drives and floppy drives.

Magneto Optical Drive – A drive that uses both magnetic and optical characteristics to store data. Examples include several removable cartridge hard drives and Minidiscs primarily used in the 1980s and 1990s.

Malware – Short for MALicious softWARE. Software primarily designed to make the author money by nefarious means such as serving up ads on your computer, stealing banking passwords, collecting information about you to be resold to data brokers, etc.

Mapped Drive – A logical drive on your computer that typically is located on another computer. For example if you have a file server you could map a drive so that it showed up on your computer as if it was actually installed in your computer.

Master Boot Record – A section at the very beginning of bootable media such as a hard drive that tells IBM compatible PCs how the hard drive is organized and also contains a boot loader (a piece of code that passes control over to the operating system).

MBR – See Master Boot Record.

Mean Time Between Failures – An average of the time between failures of a specific device. Technically it uses the mean and not an average for you math geniuses out there. Designed to show the reliability of a device. Higher MTBFs means a more reliable device while lower values show a less reliable device.

Media – Refers to anything used to store data such as a floppy disk, CD, DVD, hard drive or flash drive.

Memory – Refers to a temporary storage area in a computer or device that holds data the CPU is currently working on. More memory generally means better performance at least to the point where the CPU and primary storage media can no longer use more memory.

Memory Card – A small piece of media used in small devices such as cameras, media players (iPod etc), smart phones and tablets to store data. These can be read using a card reader. Typical types of cards include CF, SD, and microSD cards.

Microchip – An integrated circuit, or electrical circuit comprised of many electronic components such as transistors, on a single platform, generally a piece of silicon. This component is designed to function as a single unit.

Microdrive – A hard drive approximately 2"x1.4"x.4" designed to fit in a standard compact flash memory card slot.

Mini-Disc – A magneto-optical disc format used primarily for audio storage in the 1980s and 1990s but also capable for storing up to 1GB of data. Data versions were mainly used to store things such as video from surveillance systems. Audio stored on MD was CD quality in most cases and far surpassed MP3s typical of the early 1990s.

MLC – See Multi-Level Cells.

Motherboard – A term for the primary electronic board in a computer that everything else connects to such as CPU, graphics card, network card, etc. In fact, motherboards today often have many items built right into them instead of having the need of plugging in cards.

MTBF – See Mean Time Between Failure.

Multi-Level Cells – Each cell in a multi-level cell flash storage device can contain more than one bit of information. Today MLC flash storage typically stores two bits per transistor so it can store twice as much data using the same number of transistors as SLC flash storage.

NAS – See Network Attached Storage.

Network Attached Storage – A device that stores data, typically on one or more hard drives or SSDs, and allows that data to be accessed easily over a network. NAS storage devices supporting more than one storage device virtually always support RAID configurations.

New Technology File System – The replacement for the FAT file system used on Microsoft's Windows based computers. This file system was faster, more robust and allowed for larger files and larger disks than its predecessor.

NTFS – See New Technology File System.

Online Backup – The process of backing up your device to a place or service on the internet.

Operating System – Software that is designed to operate a computer system and provide services that other software can use to provide services to the user (programs).

Optical Disc – A disc that can be read from and/or written to by use of an optical medium such as a laser beam. CDs, DVDs, and BDs all are types of optical discs.

Optical Disc Drive – A drive which uses an optical medium such as a laser beam to read and/or write to an optical disc.

Overwrite – Writing new data over the top of, or where old data used to be. Once overwritten the old data cannot be recovered.

P/E Cycle – A Program /Erase Cycle is writing data to a specific bit of memory and then erasing that data off of it. Modern flash storage has a limited number of P/E cycles of life. Once a particular piece of flash memory has been through so many P/E cycles it will no longer be able to store data.

Partition – A logical division of storage media that allows a file system to be placed on it.

Patch – Generally refers to a piece of software that is updated to fix a flaw in the original program.

PBA – See Physical Block Addressing.

Pentalobe – A special type of screwdriver tip used primarily in Apple devices such as iPhones.

Photosensitive – A substance or device that reacts to light. Your skin is photosensitive in that it may darken or burn when exposed to sunlight.

Physical – Something touchable such as a hard drive. Generally used in discussions of physical and logical divisions of storage.

Physical Block Addressing – A method of translating addresses from the one requested by the computer to the one inside a storage device such as a hard drive. This change of address allows the hard drive to mark a sector as bad and remap the PBA to a new internal address. For example if PBA 123456 pointed to C5:H2:S8 (cylinder 5, head 2 and sector 8) and it was physically bad then the hard drive could remap PBA 123456 to C5:H4:S1 and requests for PBA 123456 would still function as intended. The change in location would be completely transparent.

Pirated – Taken/downloaded/used without being paid for or authorized to do so.

Pit – The lower portion of an optical disc's data surface.

Platter – A rotating disk storing data like those found inside a hard drive or in the removable cartridge of removable cartridge hard drives and magneto optical drives. These include standard hard drives, Jazz drives and MD disks.

Play Store – An online store hosted by Google containing apps for Android devices as well as video, music and books.

Podcast – An audio file typically containing some form of talk show released on a regular basis in a format that is playable in a podcast player. These players are available for virtually all platforms including iOS, Android, Windows, Mac and Linux.

Potentially Unwanted Program – A piece of software that is technically neither virus nor spyware but is typically installed in such a way that the user does not know it is being installed. These are often bundled with software such as Adobe Flash and Oracle Java which the end user does want. While normally not harmful to the computer, installation of these may slow the computer or cause confusion.

Power On – Turning a device on.

Power Supply – The part that plugs into your wall outlet and provides DC power to your computer. This can be an internal component like most desktop computers or an external component as with most laptops, tablets and smartphones.

Preboot Execution Environment – A method that allows a computer to boot from over a network instead of off of a local storage device.

Professional – Someone who does something for a living, or an item that is used by someone to earn a living. Can also refer to a particular type of license for software which will typically be used in a business environment.

Programs – Software used to manipulate data. A photograph is data while Adobe Photoshop is a program. Microsoft Word is a program which can be used to create documents which are data.

PUP – See Potentially Unwanted Program.

PXE Server – A computer and software that provides the necessary functionality to allow other computers to boot to a network boot device instead of a local storage medium.

Quad Layer – Refers to optical discs which have four different layers of reflective material in them. One layer is completely reflective and the others are semi-transparent. The device reading the disc can refocus the laser used to read the media on one layer or the other and thereby read one layer or the other. This allows the disc to store substantially more data than discs with fewer layers.

RAID – See Redundant Array of Inexpensive Disks.

RAM – See Random Access Memory.

Random Access Memory – A temporary storage location where computational work is stored between something like a CPU which does the actual computations and a long term storage device such as a hard drive. Think of it as your desk; files are stored in a filing cabinet, pulled out and placed on the desk while you work on them, then put back into the filing cabinet when you are done.

Ransomware – A virus like piece of software that infects your system in such a way as to prevent you from accessing your data until you pay the author money.

Read Error – Refers to an error that occurs when trying to read storage media such as a hard drive. This could be caused by a defect on the media, corrupt data, a bad cable, etc.

Recover – The act of getting data back that was thought to be lost.

Recycle Bin – An icon on Windows computer desktops that resembles a trash can and is used to hold unwanted items until it is emptied and the contents deleted.

Redundant Array of Inexpensive Disks – Multiple hard drives arranged in such a way that they act together for the benefit of increased speed, reliability and/or storage capacity.

Removable Media – Storage media that can be removed from a device and retain the data written to it. This includes things like memory cards, DVDs and flash drives.

Rewritable – Storage media that can be written to, erased and then written to again. Typically these can be used many times.

Root Directory – The lowest portion of a hierarchal filing system, or the starting point. The place from which everything else extends. On a DOS or Windows primary hard drive this would be represented as "C:\".

SATA – See Serial AT Attachment.

SD – See Secure Digital.

Sector – The smallest storage unit of a storage device such as a hard drive.

Secure Digital – A common type of memory card used in cameras and media players.

Self-Monitoring, Analysis, and Reporting Technology – Systems built into modern hard drives that continuously monitor the drive for problems and warns the user on boot up of the computer if there are issues.

Serial AT Attachment – The method of attaching devices such as hard drives, SSDs and optical drives that replaced the old IDE system. SATA sends data at high speed in a serial manner (one bit after another) and was originally released in 2003.

Server – In this book, refers to a computer or device set up in such a way that its primary job is to share information with other computers.

Service – A program that runs in the background at a very low level and provides services to the operating system or other programs. Examples include the print spooler service which handles print jobs and the Plug and Play service which helps load drivers for hardware that is plugged into your computer.

SFC – See System File Checker.

Shadow Copy – See Volume Snapshot Service.

Single-Level Cells – In SLC flash memory each cell of memory is a transistor that can be either on, or off. Since the transistor can only be on or off, this stores a single bit of information.

Single Layer – Refers to optical discs which have one layer of reflective material in them. This layer is completely reflective. The device reading the disc focuses the laser used to read the media on the layer to read data.

Slack – File systems are usually divided into sections which are a certain size, say 4k. If you write a file that is 5k in size that will use two 4k sections to store the file. The extra unused 3k in the second section is called slack.

SLC – See Single-Level Cells.

SMART – See Self-Monitoring, Analysis, and Reporting Technology.

Snapshot – Refers to creating a copy of a storage device as it was at a particular point in time.

Software – See Programs.

Solder – The act of heating two metal objects and then melting metal (called solder) onto them to make a solid connection between the two objects.

Solid State Drive – A storage device typically replacing a hard drive offering higher reliability and substantially faster speeds. SSDs have no moving parts and are built using flash memory instead of rotating disks. Although very reasonably priced today for the average user they are still far too expensive in sizes of 1TB and larger for most people.

Source – Refers to the drive you want to copy, or the drive containing data that you want to backup. This data is then copied to the target drive.

Spindle – The center of the hard drive where the platters rotate around.

Spindle Speed – The speed at which the platters revolve around the spindle usually expressed in RPM, revolutions per minute.

Spudger – Typically a plastic piece used to push, nudge or pry while working on small electronic devices.

Spyware – Software primarily designed to make the author money by nefarious means such as serving up ads on your computer, stealing banking passwords, collecting information on you to be resold to data brokers, etc.

SSD – See Solid State Drive.

Storage Device – Any device used to store programs and/or data that maintains the information without the need for power.

Stream – The process of a continuous flow of data from the internet to a device or piece of software where it is played as it is being downloaded instead of waiting for the download to complete before playback is possible. Watching a movie or listening to music from the internet is typically done streaming.

Synchronize – To make two things exactly the same. Often used in backup programs to make the backup an exact copy of the original.

System File Checker – A program build into Windows that checks the operating system for corrupt, missing or incorrect files.

Tape Drive – A backup device using tapes to store data. These tapes are very roughly similar in idea to the old cassette tapes.

Target - Refers to the drive you want to make a copy to, or the drive where you want your data backed up to. This data is copied from the source drive.

Task – In the context of computers a task is a job the computer will do and is either scheduled or manually executed by means of some icon or task management program. Windows includes a Task Scheduler just for running tasks like cleanups, backups, updates, etc.

Terminal – On a MacOS or Linux computer it is a program that allows you to directly type commands to the operating system without using a mouse or graphics of any kind.

Third Party – Someone other than the manufacturer of the device. For example if you purchase a charging cable from Apple for your iPhone that is not third party. If however you buy the Amazon Basics version from Amazon.com that would be a third party cable.

Thumb Drive – A name for a small portable USB flash storage device.

Thunderbolt – A method of connecting external components, such as an external hard drive, to a computer similar to USB. These are predominately found on Macintosh computers and can transfer data at speeds of 40 Gb/sec.

Torx – A type of screwdriver bit often used when working on Apple devices and computers.

Track – All the sectors in a concentric ring of a data storage platter such as in a hard drive are considered to be on the same logical track.

TRIM – A command set that allows Solid State Drives to perform deletes in a more efficient manner which does not reduce the life of the drive by increasing the P/E cycle count. It must be supported by both the SSD and operating system although all modern operating systems and SSDs do.

Turntable – A device that spins an album, usually made of vinyl, which has a needle on an arm. This needle contacts the album and as it hits irregularities this makes sounds which are then sent to an amplification device and eventually to speakers.

UEFI - See Unified Extensible Firmware Interface.

UHD Premium – Ultra High Definition Premium. A specification released by the UHD Alliance that defines the resolution, bit depth, color pallet, brightness levels and more that must be present in a device in order to display the UHD Premium logo. This ensures you are getting a certain level of performance and that whatever you are buying is compatible with everything else carrying the logo.

Unified Extensible Firmware Interface – A replacement for the BIOS on computers that provides a bridge between the hardware of the computer and the bootable portions of the operating system.

Universal Serial Bus – A system for connecting components to a computer (generally external devices) allowing for speeds up to 12Mb/sec. This is sometimes referred to as USB1.1.

Update – Refers to a newer version of something. For example if Microsoft Windows releases an update that would replace current files with newer versions which offer some improvement, generally a fix of a security problem, improved performance or repair of a defect.

USB – See Universal Serial Bus.

USB2 - Also called High-Speed USB it is the second generation of USB specifications. It is backwards compatible with previous USB specifications. USB2 can transfer data at speeds of up to 280 Mb/sec.

USB3 – Also called SuperSpeed USB it is the third generation of USB specifications. It is backwards compatible with previous USB specifications. USB3 can transfer data at speeds of up to 5 Gb/sec.

USB Drive – See USB Flash Drive.

USB Flash Drive – A name for a small portable USB flash storage device.

Ultra Violet Light – A part of the spectrum of light emitted primarily by the sun (and tanning booths) which can harm optical discs.

UV Light – See Ultra Violet Light.

User Error – An error that was caused by the actions of the person operating the device and not a malfunction of the device.

Versioning – A method of keeping multiple backups of a file, making a new backup each time the file is changed without deleting or removing the older backup. This helps protect against file corruption or infection so if the last version is not usable, one can restore a previous version.

Virus – A piece of software whose primary job is to self-replicate and do damage. Damage could be simply deleting files, entire file systems, or preventing the use of the computer.

Volume Snapshot Service – A service in Microsoft's Windows operating system that allows for automatically or manually taking a "snapshot", or copy, of a file while it is in use. This technology is used by backup programs and Windows to make backups and/or restore points without the need of turning off the computer or stopping work. This service requires the use of the NTFS file system.

VSS – See Volume Snapshot Service.

Wear Leveling – The process used by an SSD to equalize the wear on all parts of the unit as best as possible. Since the memory used in SSDs can only be written to so many times, wear leveling can substantially increase the usable life of the drive.

Windows – An operating system developed by Microsoft for use on IBM compatible PCs.

Word – An organizational unit of data containing 8, 16, 32 or 64 bits of data.

Write Error – Refers to an error that occurs when trying to write to storage media such as a hard drive. This could be caused by a defect on the media, corrupt data, a bad cable, etc.

Writable – Typically refers to optical media that the end user can write data to.

Zip Drive – A drive manufactured starting in the 1990s by Iomega containing basically a large, high capacity floppy drive. These could be connected by IDE, parallel, SCSI, USB or Firewire to a computer and came in sizes including 100MB, 250MB and finally 750MB.

Part 10: Other books by the author

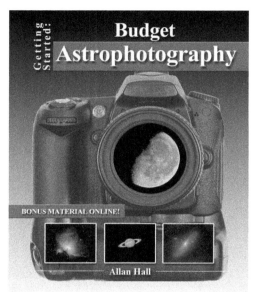

Want to take a few snapshots of the beautiful objects you are viewing without spending a small fortune? Already have a camera but you can't seem to get a good image and want to know why?

This book will answer those and many other questions while giving you a quick and reasonably easy introduction to budget astrophotography. In addition, save more money by seeing how to make a lot of items you may find useful.

http://www.allans-stuff.com/bap/

If you decide that you want more than quick snapshots, you want big beautiful prints to hang on your wall, this is the book for you.

From required and optional equipment, through the capture process and into the software processing needed to create outstanding images, this book will walk you through it all.

http://www.allans-stuff.com/leap/

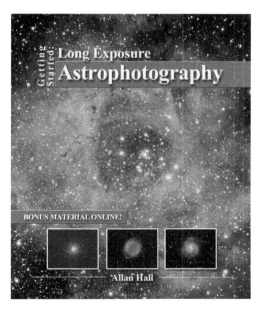

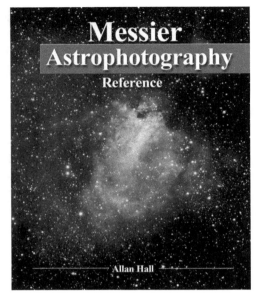

You decide that you want to take images of celestial targets, but need a little help with the targets? This book discusses all 110 Messier targets and includes descriptions, realistic images of each target, star charts and shoot notes to help you image all 110 of the objects yourself.

http://www.allans-stuff.com/mar/

If you have ever wanted to view the wondrous objects of our solar system and beyond, here is the how-to manual to get you well on your way. From purchasing your first telescope, through setting it up and finding objects, to viewing your first galaxy, this book contains everything you need. Learn how to read star maps and navigate the celestial sphere and much more with plenty of pictures, diagrams and charts to make it easy. Written specifically for the novice and assuming the reader has no knowledge of astronomy makes sure that all topics are explained thoroughly from the ground up. Use this book to

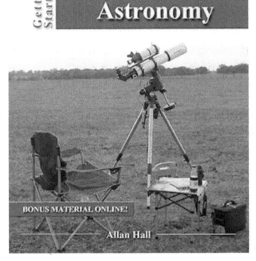

embark on a fantastic new hobby and learn about the universe at the same time!

http://www.allans-stuff.com/va/

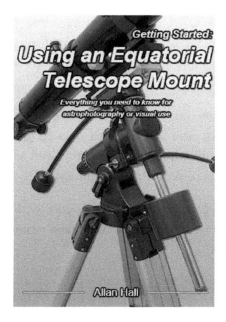

Many midrange and high end telescopes come on equatorial mounts. These mounts are fantastic for tracking celestial objects. Someone who wanted to take pictures of objects in the night sky might even say they are required for all but the most basic astrophotography. The problem is that they can also be unintuitive and require some knowledge to use.

If you have ever struggled to figure out how to use an equatorial telescope mount, this is the book you always wished you had.

http://www.allans-stuff.com/eq/

So you've decided to write a book and get into non-fiction publishing. Now you find yourself faced with the seemingly infinitely harder second step – actually bringing the idea to market. In today's brave new world of self-publishing and open creative markets, it is both an inviting and potentially intimidating arena for authors hoping to turn their non-fiction books into a meaningful source of income. This is a daunting task because it involves a blend of several disciplines that aren't necessarily part of an author's quiver of arrows. Most crucial among these are marketing and digital publishing, each of which requires fluency in fields that authors may or may not have experience in.

http://www.allans-stuff.com/ck/

If you have every wanted to see why WordPress is one of the most popular website platforms today but didn't know where to start, this book is for you.

Starting off with no knowledge of websites, hosting, or HTML you will learn to how to get your own domain name and web host as well as install and configure WordPress from scratch.

It doesn't stop there, you will then work with plugins, widgets, and themes to make your website shine.

http://www.allans-stuff.com/wpress

NOTES:

NOTES:

www.ingramcontent.com/pod-product-compliance
Lightning Source LLC
Chambersburg PA
CBHW060543060326
40690CB00017B/3590